PAULA DEERING

PAULA DEERING

DINING
BY
DESIGN

DINING BY DESIGN

Interior Design's Handbook of Dining and Restaurant Facilities

By Edie Lee Cohen and Sherman R. Emery

INTERIOR
DESIGN
BOOKS

Published by
CAHNERS PUBLISHING COMPANY
475 Park Avenue South, New York, NY 10016

Distributed by
VAN NOSTRAND REINHOLD COMPANY
135 West 50th Street, New York NY 10020

To Virginia Evans and Chris Duffy
without whose help this book would not
have been possible

First published in USA by
Cahners Publishing Company
475 Park Avenue South, New York, NY 10016

Designed by Stuart Handelman and Janet Czarnetzki

Publications Manager: Christine Duffy

Printed and bound in Japan by Dai Nippon Printing Company
through DNP (America), Inc.

Distributed to the trade by
Van Nostrand Reinhold Company, Inc.
135 West 50th Street, New York, NY 10020

Library of Congress Cataloging in Publication Data

Cohen, Edie Lee, 1950-
    Dining by design.

    Includes index.
    1. Restaurants, lunch rooms, etc.—United States—
Decorations. 2. Interior decoration—United States—
History—20th century. I. Emery, Sherman R.
II. Title.
NK2195.R4C63 1984   725'.71'0973   84-12167
ISBN 0-943370-04-3

10 9 8 7 6 5 4 3 2 1

Introduction

What makes a successful restaurant? It is not always easy to determine. A four-star review in *The New York Times* will ensure success—at least for a time. But as our case study of *The Grand Cafe* at the end of this book shows, four-star ratings are not enough if management fails to maintain its original standards.

Eating out today is big business. According to one report, the fast-food business is the third largest in America. Yet restaurants probably have one of the highest mortality rates in the country. It is obvious, then, that much more is needed than gut intuition, good taste and a developed palette to create that special mystique that marks a successful dining facility.

In talking to dozens of designers and restaurant specialists, we find a general agreement. There is no magic formula. Restaurateur Joseph Baum says: "There are no pat formulas to use. Formulas lead not to solutions, but only to clichés. And clichés lead only to obsolescence."

There are, however, important guidelines which can help steer the interior designer and restaurateur in the right direction. And that is what this book is all about: a compendium of well-designed restaurants and descriptions of how they were conceived, with special sections devoted to such all-important subjects as lighting, acoustics, graphics and budgets—all told through in-depth interviews with experts in those fields.

One of the designer's major roles in helping to create a successful restaurant is to provide the ambience—the mood, the atmosphere—those elements which often make the difference between a place merely to "eat out" and one that provides the experience of "dining out." For as most experts agree, people eat out today not just for the food but for the entertainment and for the experience of celebration. Dining out has become a social phenomenon.

It is a combination of factors, then, that lead to a successful restaurant; design, service and food must all work together. More often than not, the successful restaurant is one in which the designer, client and restaurateur have dared to take risks. Not necessarily outrageous. Not necessarily flamboyant. Just enough risks so that the particular restaurant they've created breaks out of the expected mold. We hope that the projects shown in this book will inspire others to take those risks.

Edie Lee Cohen   **Sherman R. Emery**

Table of Contents

Foreword by George Lang

Although the art of cooking and hospitality in exchange for payment is ages old, the restaurant has not been with us very long. As a business and as a social institution, the restaurant had its origin in a number of relatively recent developments: the French Revolution, the increasing urbanization of people, technological advances and the growth of the middle classes with their leisure and status demands. But the restaurant mostly owes its birth and development to the national genius of France.

In the United States, the 200-year-old restaurant industry has been additionally affected by what historian Daniel Boorstin calls the "American experience": democracy, vast spaces, unlimited resources, and faster transportation pushing people and goods farther. This, plus a "go-getting climate" and a "search for novelty," has brought the level of our restaurants to a unique position.

Today we live in an age of rapidly growing expectations, but in the distant past, the Neanderthal man probably felt as if he were surrounded with luxury when he found a flat stone on which to sit; decoration was provided by nature, and when his wife served some of his food on leaves and shells, the age of gracious living began.

Still, it was a long way to the Persian court, where the dining rooms of the wealthy were lined with porphyry, alabaster and carpet hangings, and courtesans, dancers and other practitioners of the lively arts graced the proceedings.

The Romans, as usual, outdid everyone else. In the houses of the more ostentatious noblemen, the guests changed tables for every course, and each table was decorated according to the food it held. Servants stood with torches throughout the night, so no blackout problems were reported. As the lady guests indulged in wine, footmen held perfumed silk cloths in front of them to prevent stains on their dresses.

The concept of public eating establishments did not come readily to mankind. For centuries, travelers who were forced to eat away from home carried with them their own food supplies, which were supplemented by buying the staples of life en route.

When food is precious, it is hoarded, not sold, so restaurants had to depend on the operation of the laws of supply as well as demand. As Omar Khayyám said:

"I wonder often what the Vintners buy
One half as precious as the stuff they sell."

France, abundantly blessed with harvests, was perhaps a logical place for the true restaurant to begin and especially in Paris, its capital.

The rise of the bourgeoisie during and after the French Revolution of 1789 provided an adequate boost to the restaurant concept as we know it. The public demanded meeting places that served food and wine in a handsome, comfortable atmosphere. The chefs from the aristocratic kitchens were readily available after *they* lost their jobs (and their employers lost their heads); the restaurant business was on its way.

Many authorities award the designation of being the first restaurateur to Monsieur Boulanger of Paris, who in 1765 started to dispense a nourishing and restorative soup. His business flourished, even though Louis XV, a self-proclaimed gourmet, considered the soups to be "inedible," thus becoming the first professional, though unpaid, restaurant critic.

M. Boulanger's apt descriptive term "restaurant," which adapted from the French means restorant, caught on and was adopted all over Europe as the international word restaurant. Soon, restaurants with luxurious appointments designed by the greatest architects, with impeccable service, superb food and wine, appeared throughout the city of Paris.

Many authors have viewed the social history of France in the 19th century as it is mirrored in its restaurants. Here is a contemporary description of the Grand Cafe Parisien:

"A splendor to make one dizzy. It is not just a cafe: it is a temple. One enters an enchanted palace of the 1000 nights; a dazzlement in which the artistic magnificence is carried to its extreme limits."

The architects and designers already understood the importance of the total concept, delighting at the same time in supportive details. The design of these cafes reflected the other arts of Paris: the music of Offenbach and the artistry of Renoir and Toulouse-Lautrec, who illustrated the luxurious menus.

The 20th century brought even more far-reaching changes to the dining room. First of all, greater quantities of natural or electric light could be added to dark and somber areas, and chair designers became more aware of the human shape.

What direction should a designer take today?

I came up with the answer during an interminable cross-country flight. The restaurants of my choice have imperfections, but they all make me divinely happy.

In our Alice in Wonderland–type country, how does one stay in one place or get ahead?

I think the Red Queen whispers into our ears if we listen:

1. Analyze, plan, set up equations of problems and solutions, i.e., "method merchandise."

2. As a designer, you must work with the architects, the restaurateurs and perhaps with professional consultants who train themselves how to sidestep the obstacles of the past while traveling carefully among the limited possibilities of the future.

3. You must simultaneously solve the cosmic Catch-22, i.e., how to be a searching, comparing, scholarly analyst and, at the same time, with the awareness of the above (perhaps using it as an invisible guideline), how to let go and allow your imagination to take over.

4. You must understand that the act of creation must be within a well-defined process because, while it's true that there is a market for every restaurant, an incorrectly conceived and designed specimen won't last long enough to be able to find it. You, as designer, are partly responsible for this search.

5. You have to believe that today's consumer is more sophisticated than yesterday's, and the public in general is less attracted to the artificial, and more resistant to newness for its own sake.

6. To be successful in creating concepts for the hospitality industry—as in any form of marketing—the designer must have a finger on the pulse of the times as much as a social historian does.

7. Designers may think they are safe in copying earlier successful concepts (even their own) but will find that the new version fails because an idea that worked at one time and in one particular location will not necessarily translate to another.

8. Above all, avoid those cheap easy tricks and derivative details that are supposed to marry "modern" to "traditional," but are only a signal of failure of conviction and creativity, as Ada Louise Huxtable said a few years ago.

9. If you want to design a restaurant which the guest will enjoy, you have to create a restaurant that you'll enjoy, and one that will be an intelligent setting for the hedonistic pleasures of the white table.

10. You must be able to see the amusing side of things and not take yourself too seriously. Solemnity is only an olive's throw from pompousness.

The face we put on our designs should be our own face and the smile must be more than just the motion of the orbicular muscles.

William J. Smith said, "Laughter animates the business of life; it makes things happen. It creates varied, multi-colored existence. It gives us a world not rigid and heavy but shifting, ever-changing and light."

Merriment does have, however, a mercurial quality and if we understand this, we will understand the true appreciation of pleasure and the natural science of giving pleasure to people.

Dining is a business like no other business, and designing a restaurant is like no other design job. The designer must fulfill every guest's personal fantasies in a single interior which at the same time will have to be a modern counterpart of the Greek agora, a place of recreation for everyone present.

One must come to the conclusion that, although we eat in order to live, we also want to enjoy this essentially biological process. This is where our designers enter and gather their talents around the legitimate task of creating spaces which are conducive to the convivial consumption of food and beverages.

The practitioners of this art and applied art form in this book are all taking a stand against the disposable culture. Since we are eagerly obliterating our finest hotels and restaurants, their work is especially vital today.

Tradition is as essential to our visual world as foundations are to a building, but often tradition is used by over-conservative arbiters of taste as a form of conspiracy in order to keep the future from happening.

The generation that was born before the Great Depression feels nostalgic about a world at which they only glimpsed, and today's younger generation fantasizes about the past by reviving old movies and fashions and encouraging designers to fake stage-set versions of restaurants of the past.

Although one cannot return to the actual past, there is an increasing desire to cherish our heritage and maintain a continuity with earlier ways of life. This wistful yearning can be turned into today's images by sensitive designers.

The world of restaurant design is littered with broken clichés and broken leases because the act of improvisation or desperation is often substituted for the act of creation. I represent the small fraternity that believes in considering the total picture before deciding on the goal and the road toward this goal. Perhaps our professional bible should say: "In the beginning, there was the feasibility study."

The composers of the 18th and 19th centuries often took a well-known theme, each doing his own variation on it, each ending up with a different piece, and every one of them retaining its own validity. Whether you are part of the Old Guard or New Breed, your design can bear the profile of its creator based on your particular talents and skills.

Restaurant design is a compromise with impossibilities, but when you eliminate the impossible, what remains is the truth.

In this book many very talented people are discussing their own kinds of truths, and in this ongoing shell game, anyone can be right, provided that he is not wrong.

Windows on the World

WINDOWS ON THE WORLD

Location: New York, New York
Seating Capacity: 350 (main dining room)
Interior Designer: Warren Platner Associates
Photographers: Ezra Stoller, Alexandre Georges, Jaime Ardiles-Arce

After eight years, WINDOWS ON THE WORLD is still one of New York's main tourist attractions, and according to its director, Alan Lewis, the project not only meets but also exceeds its original expectations and continues to set records.

What is its appeal? There are, of course, the spectacular views from the 107th floor of Number One World Trade Center—views that encompass New York Harbor, the Statue of Liberty and most of Manhattan.

But there is also the ambience and the feeling of being in a place that is "special," qualities all attributable to the masterful interior design and planning of Warren Platner who literally turned an acre of space, in what is basically an office building, into one of the most successful restaurants in New York.

The first step in the planning was the decision to use the entire perimeter of the floor for dining, thus giving patrons full advantage of the views from the windows. Service areas are relegated to the interior core of the building where they are fitted into the left-over spaces between duct shaft, fire stairs, diagonal bracing and the like.

The next major decision was to terrace the main dining space so that the farther away one sits from the windows, the higher he is. This gives everyone a choice location. The largest dining spaces are placed at the four corners of the building, thus giving diners there a double view.

Although the space is vast in scale, a feeling of intimacy has been achieved throughout. Even in the main dining room, which seats 350, guests are not lined up in rows as they are in most New York restaurants, but seated in a private alcove or on a terrace.

Platner's design concept was that any decorations used must be meaningful and not just visually appealing. This premise is especially evident in the spectacular glass-and-mirror entrance gallery, a long (65') narrow space which leads visitors from the reception room to the public dining spaces. It is a true *tour de force* of design, and the effect of walking through the passage is

Reception room is intimately scaled, the low ceiling achieved by elevating the floor. The wall behind the reception desk faces the elevators and captures attention with its gold-leafed design; fresh flowers are reflected in a kaleidoscopic construction of angled mirrors projecting from the end wall.

13

To enter the dining rooms, guests must cross a 65'
long gallery with a mirrored ceiling and partially
mirrored walls. Photographic images of world scenes
are arranged in panels and set between the mirrors
and glass arches which subdivide the space. By
alternating photographic perspective with mirrors and
clear glass, the designers have created an illusory
feeling of great depth. Four large semi-precious stones
rest on brass pedestals in the passageway. Reflected
light from the walls and ceiling light the space and
people passing through it.

Special glass: Metralite. *Semi-precious stones*: Ludlow Smith
& Cann. *Lighting*: Lightolier. *Pedestals*: Melto Metals. *Mirrors*:
James Catalano & Sons. *General contractor*: Dember
Construction Co.

somewhat like that of being inside a kaleidoscope. The theme is international with images of cities and civilization from around the world. Symbolically representing the four corners of the earth are four large semi-precious stones, each from a different continent.

There are 17 private dining rooms that seat from four to six in the smaller ones, or as many as 150 in a combination of several adjoining spaces. For flexibility of use, the rooms are arranged in hotel banquet room fashion with folding walls between. All have standard acoustical tile ceilings and cream colored painted plasterboard walls. The main decorative themes are traditional symbols of hospitality such as fruit and flowers.

The total working budget for the project was set at six and one half million dollars, a figure which included two million for mechanical systems, air conditioning, plumbing and basic electrical work. Part of the basic budget was used to elevate the floors and create a terraced space in the main dining room. Inexpensive materials, such as plaster board and stock acoustical tile ceilings, were used in large quantities, and expensive materials such as marble and gold ceramic tile for columns in the dining room were specified in small quantities.

In addition to his staff, Platner singles out one man who helped create a smooth operation enabling the restaurant to serve hundreds of people without a hitch every day—the restaurant specialist, Joseph Baum.

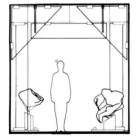

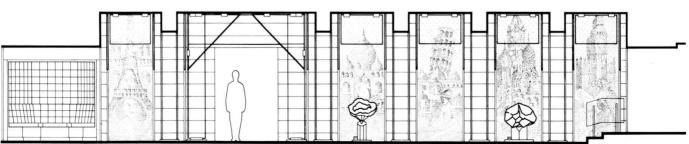

*The teak bar in The Grill area of Windows rests on a
black and white marble base and measures 38' in
length; above it is a vaulted ceiling of faceted mirror,
and to the left is a teak leaning rail enabling people
to enjoy the view while standing and drinking.*

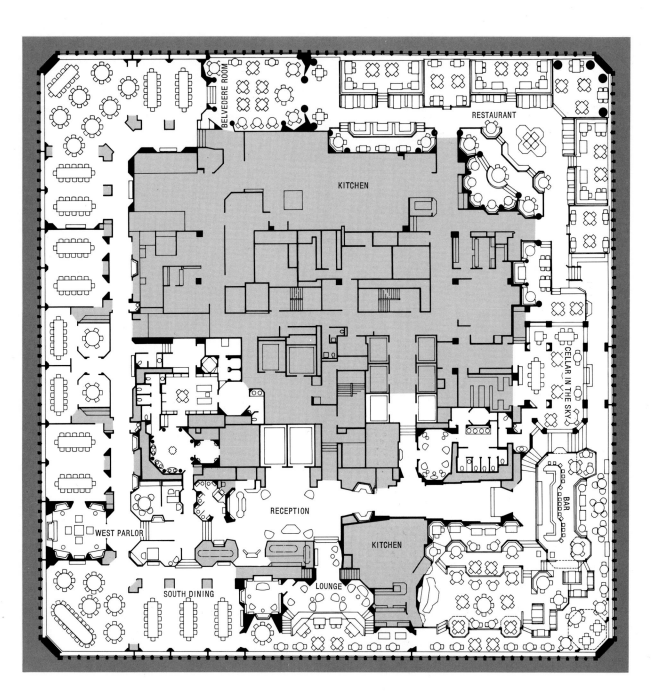

The main dining room occupies one of the four corners of the building and is tiered toward the windows offering diners spectacular views of Manhattan and Brooklyn. Vertical cylinders, covered with custom gold ceramic tile, are placed at the outer corner and repeated at the west end of the space. Strips of mirror across the back of banquettes enable guests to see the view even if they are not facing the windows.

Carpet: Brintons. *Wood flooring*: Bangkok Industries. *Plastic laminate, walls, window mullions*: Wilson Art. *Gold ceramic tile*: Designers Tile International. *Dining chairs*: Stendig. *Glassware*: Louie Glass Co. *Crystal*: Lenox. *China*: Rosenthal. *Silverware*: Reed and Barton. *Linens*: James G. Hardy.

There are 17 private dining rooms at Windows on the World which seat from four to six in the smaller ones, or as many as 150 in a combination of several adjoining spaces. Artwork and decoration provide individuality and variety, two of the main motifs being fruits and flowers to symbolize hospitality. Tulips provide the theme in the room shown here: at left, a painting by Susan Leites; in the overall view of the room shown on the facing page, color enlargements from photographs by Alexandre Georges.

Chairs: Lehigh/Leopold. *Upholstery fabric*: Timme. *Photo printing*: Chromeprint. *Special framing*: Juno Woodworking.

The women's powder room measures 12' x 17' with
only an 8' ceiling; it gains greater depth from a
faceted-mirror lining, interrupted by a large panel of
silk embroidery. Lighting consists of exposed bulbs
above the mirrors.

Carpet: Brintons. *Wall fabric*: Jack Lenor Larsen. *Stools*:
Knoll. *Bulbs*: Durotest.

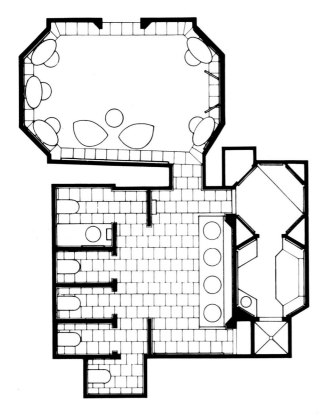

LE RENDEZ-VOUS

Location: Chicago, Illinois
Seating Capacity: 68 (first floor); 52 (third floor)
Interior Designer: Spiros Zakas, Zakaspace
Photographer: Idaka

In a three-level facility that would include a restaurant, cocktail lounge and bar, the client requested an ambience that would resemble a French country club. The building selected for the project was of Victorian vintage that had at one time been used as a pizza restaurant.

To create new backgrounds, the designer completely gutted the space and extended the facade to add a glass frame that would create a more dramatic entrance. An open stairway built over a planted area leads guests directly to the second floor where the lounge and bar are located. Above and below this are the dining rooms. The one on the first floor is divided into sections with divisions between every two tables for people who want more of a feeling of seclusion. The top floor is where people come to see and be seen. Here, the space is more open, and all the tables can be viewed as one enters. Each floor has its own carpet pattern and color scheme, but a feeling of unity is maintained throughout with the repetition of architectural columns and paneling.

Interior construction: Jerry Pascal & Associates. *Booth chairs:* Metropolitan. *Fabrics:* Stroheim & Romann. *Lighting fixtures:* Castelli. *Mirror:* Midwest Glass.

Entrance to the restaurant is shown at right; an open stairway leads guests to the second level where the bar/lounge is located. On the facing page is a detail view of banquette seating in an alcove area on the third floor.

First Floor

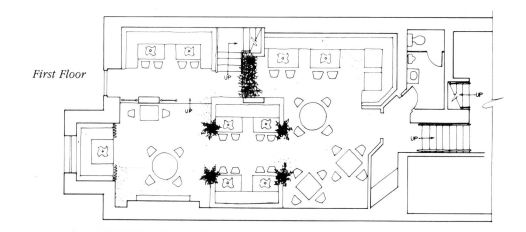

The two views on this page and at the top of the facing page are of the first floor dining room which offers more secluded dining with divisions between every two tables; a mirrored wall helps to expand the space visually. The third floor dining room (bottom photograph, opposite page) is completely open; walls are covered with shirred fabric and accented with Art Deco paintings from a French theater.

Third Floor

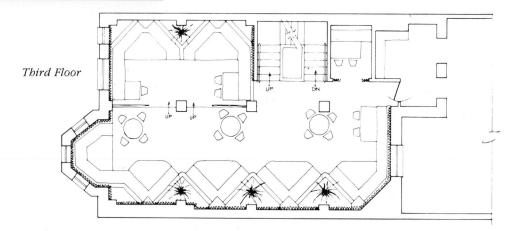

The Restaurant Consultants: George Lang and Joseph Baum

Just what is a restaurateur? In part, he is: consultant, showman, designer, marketing expert, salesman, conceptualist and gourmet. Perhaps, most importantly, he is the professional client. Broad conclusions these, arrived at after lengthy conversations with the nation's two foremost authorities, George Lang and Joseph Baum.

As background, the restaurant consultant is a relatively recent phenomenon. Historically, during the 19th and early 20th centuries, the owner established the concept and implemented it in freestanding facilities. Or, if the restaurant were part of a hotel, the end product usually resulted as a collaborative effort among the chef who created the menu, the maitre d'hotel who set up the room, and the client as overseer. But, as Lang explains, this new profession was due to arrive for a number of reasons. First, we live in an increasingly cost-oriented era where every square foot of a business must bring in a certain amount of money. The relationship between escalating costs and income is becoming more difficult to live with; somehow, the businessman has to transfer some expenses to his clientele. Further, competition is fierce, and an increasingly sophisticated American public wants more value for their money. Finally, he says, "The people who can execute ideas in a restaurant, both design and food-wise were becoming scarce." The time had come for the specialist who was a direct part of neither the restaurant's ownership nor its management—someone who could make decisions with no vested interests.

In a word, the restaurant consultant's main role is that of manager, one who sees connections among operations involved and puts them into the proper balance and context. Or, as Baum puts it: "We see ourselves as professional clients who analyze the problems, the demographics, who discover the market, develop criteria for a solution, create the conceptual context, write a program and then work with the designer to produce a functional operating plan."

Before any design related decisions are considered, the consultant may be called in to develop marketing/feasibility studies. "Many times," says Lang, "the consultant is brought in to prepare a study so that the corporation has a better chance of getting money from a bank or other syndicate." Or, the consultant may be called in to propose image-altering plans for existing facilities.

Teamwork is rarely without its problems. Put together client, architect, designer and consultant, and the potential for disaster seems particularly great. To avoid it, there must be a clear definition of roles and acceptance of the others' expertise. The procedure of what comes first must be agreed upon by all. Speaking of the designer's role, Baum comments that the designer must be reponsible to the consultant as well. Elaborating on this definition of roles, Lang makes the analogy: "I think the architect produces the edifice which we could call the chicken coop. The interior designer designs its interior. The restaurateur, then, will invent the chicken which continually is going to give the golden egg. Without producing the proper chicken, you have nothing but a structure with a splendid interior."

Thus, the restaurateur neither *is* nor *pretends* to be a designer. Yet he is involved in all design related decisions as they pertain to concept and operations. He advises on adjacency plans, seating configurations, perhaps kitchen design as does Lang, who has been a professional chef, perhaps specification of certain elements. The consultant also helps develop the framework for responsibilities, the timing schedule and the approximate budget for each stage. He collaborates with the project manager, designer and other consultants to develop bid packages. Then, based on prior market research and current project costs, he may project profits for the first and following years, as well as offer ideas on expansion potential and tie-ins with other companies.

"What we're getting at," says Baum, "is how we want people to feel in specific situations, not merely what we want them to look at. We define all of this for the designer. Our work is to make the designer's solution feasible within that plan, maintaining the function of the plan while preserving the design aesthetic." The end result of a harmonious collaboration, both agree, is one where there is no distinction made among the contributors of ideas. It is a perception that the restaurant could not have been designed in any other way. "There's nothing in Windows on the World, for example, that Platner didn't want," says Baum.

Concept, aesthetics, execution aside, the consultant also influences systems, operations and service. This last, along with menu, is a key determinant of success. Through his personal network, the restaurateur is well qualified to find key personnel. But if this be the case, Lang cautions, it should be part of the contract and not expected gratis. The restaurateur often oversees training operations—teaching, explaining and instilling a vital feeling of importance in every member of the staff. There are only a few weeks in which to perfect operations, Lang comments. For usually after the third week the critic arrives, penning a review that may well spell success or portend doom.

Although there are no formulas for success, there are some outright taboos. One is to be patronizing to the clientele. Another, says Baum, "is to design anything manipulatively uncomfortable and for profit." Still another caveat is designing for oneself, not the projected market. Planning an establishment with a too sophisticated menu or wrong price structure is destined for failure. So is planning a restaurant that is out of touch with the times.

Instead, the consultant must be able to take an accurate pulse reading of the present with an eye to what will succeed in the future. "The consultant," says Lang, "if important enough within the industry, often has a double-action role. By predicting something, he will help make it happen." And from Baum: "The challenge is to properly interpret the present, understand its essences and then produce solutions and design executions that are so absoutely right for their times that their specific psychological ambience points directly towards the future."

JOSEPH BAUM is head of the Joseph Baum Corporation, along with Michael Whiteman. The corporation is a master planning/consulting firm engaged in the conceptual development, design management and implementation of major food service projects and urban retail centers.

GEORGE LANG, owner and creator of Manhattan's Cafe des Artistes, has led a multi-faceted career including: concert violinist, chef, author, columnist, television commentator and product designer.

The Architectural Approach

WOODS RESTAURANT

Location: New York, New York
Seating Capacity: 70 (dining); 20 (bar)
Interior Designers: James D'Auria and Charles Boxenbaum
Photographer: Norman McGrath

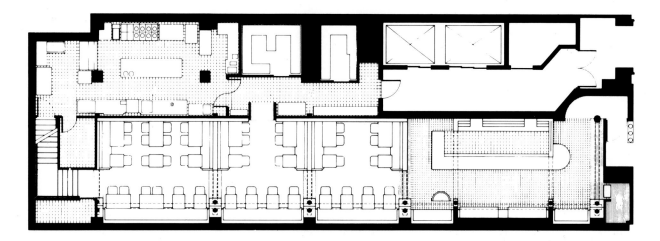

In the view on the facing page, acoustical baffles made of quilted flannel with fiberfilling are used to help absorb sound; they are suspended from an industrial track which also holds lighting fixtures. The full-length view of the dining room on the following spread shows how painted columns and overhead beams define areas without physically separating them.

This is the second restaurant with the same name to open in New York, the first being on Madison Avenue. Both are owned and operated by the same proprietor, Zeus Goldberg. This West 37th Street facility, which opened in 1981, is in the heart of the fashion industry and occupies a tunnel-like space that once housed a 1930's vintage coffee shop. To minimize the narrow box effect of the space, which measures 98' × 16½', with a 16½' ceiling, the designers left the kitchen in its rear location and broke up the length by implied rather than physical separations. This was achieved by the use of non-supporting wood columns and overhead beams, painted red, plus varying floor covering textures. These elements divide the space into logical segments from entry to coat-checking to bar-meal-counters to three successive dining rooms.

To help absorb sound, baffles made of quilted flannel, sandwiching layers of Dacron fiberfill, are suspended from the ceiling. This material, like all the fabrics throughout, were treated with Scotchgard and flameproofed. Overhead track lighting is supplemented by special illumination focusing on one wall dedicated to changing displays of photography.

So successful has Woods II proved to be that an extension is currently being planned, and a third Woods is scheduled to open in the Gramercy Park area.

General contractor: Bronx Store. *Wood flooring:* Designed Wood Flooring. *Carpet tiles:* Interface Flooring Systems. *Custom banquettes and chairs:* Empire State Chair. *Plastic laminates:* Formica. *Lighting:* Lightolier.

GEORGE'S

Location: Chicago, Illinois
Seating Capacity: 165 (dining room); 40 (lounge)
Interior Designer: Chicago Art and Architecture
Photographer: Jaime Ardiles-Arce

The location is a century-old factory in which the designers were asked to create a combination restaurant and cabaret that would attract visitors from the nearby Merchandise Mart. The area, measuring 40' × 100', is split by a row of massive columns which determined the division of the space: one side becomes the dining room and cabaret; the remainder accommodates the circulation spine, a lounge and stand-up bar. Seating in the dining area is terraced so that patrons have an unbroken view of the cabaret stage.

Backgrounds are neutral with accents of green coming from the back-illuminated glass brick wall at one end; the same material is repeated along the serpentine-shaped bar.

Carpet: Wellco: *Chairs:* Virco: *Bar and table tops:* Milwaukee Marble. *Upholstery:* Knoll.

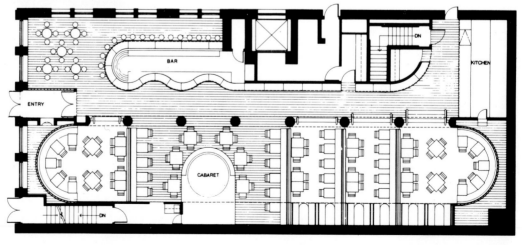

CITY BITES

Location: Philadelphia, Pennsylvania
Seating Capacity: 250
Interior Designer: Edwin Bronstein, AIA
Photographer: Courtney Winston

Viewing the movie *Starstruck*, looking at David Hockney paintings and listening to New Wave music is scarcely the stuff of which the usual design briefing is made. But this is exactly what Edwin Bronstein, AIA, and the client—an established restaurateur with whom Bronstein had worked over the past ten years—did. The client, says Bronstein, "was ready for the big risk. This was to be a restaurant that was fun, different and on the cutting edge of what is aesthetically acceptable."

Bronstein was confronted with a strict ten-week time frame and design problems inherent to the 7488-square-foot space. The time limit meant that elements had to be custom designed even while the interiors were being renovated. The space itself, formerly a restaurant, already had a centrally located kitchen. To cut time and expenses, Bronstein opted to

A windowless narrow corridor leading from the rear entry to the prime up-front seating area appears even more so with dark blue paint and enclosed booths. The booths, all with irregularly shaped backs and cutouts, are assembled on a perspective-distorting angle. The faux marbre *lintel complements the marble floor.*

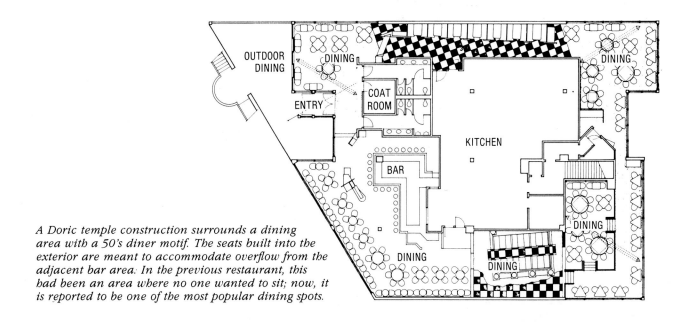

A Doric temple construction surrounds a dining area with a 50's diner motif. The seats built into the exterior are meant to accommodate overflow from the adjacent bar area. In the previous restaurant, this had been an area where no one wanted to sit; now, it is reported to be one of the most popular dining spots.

work around the existing floor plan that had the front-of-the-house space snaked around the perimeter. The main problem concerned traffic flow, with the entry at the rear of the space and the prime seating area along the glass front. How to move people through two uninteresting corridors to this up-front zone posed the difficulty.

The solution centered on the environments created in each hallway. A narrow, windowless passage was darkened with blue paint and made to appear even more narrow with an assemblage of booths along a perspective distorting angle. The second passageway, an area with a high ceiling and clerestory windows, became a Doric-columned

The most desirable seating area is upfront (left) where the glass elevation looks out to river views. The window covering, easily adjustable by patrons, is flameproof ballooning fabric, as is that in the metal structure. To the left of the console (opposite page) is the refinished bar and lounge seating. Chain link fencing is a novel display vehicle for art.

temple in which the dining environment was filled with 50's diner imagery.

The bar, existing but refinished, is adjacent to the temple. Continuing the progression, one reaches the desirable front zone. All tables at the windows are triangular shaped deuces, while those stepped back but still with access to the views are for larger parties. The black metal structure that defines this front environment was a quick and cost effective way to add supplementary lighting fixtures to the existing scheme.

With its bright, sometimes garish colors, bizarre imagery and art that may require explanation, City Bites is very much of a particular culture at a particular time. Indeed, its very trendiness—so appealing in its diversity now—may ultimately make the place look dated and contribute to its demise. Bronstein acknowledges the supposition. "We realize that it will have a short life—maybe three or four years, but that's O.K."

General contractor: Ron Markee. *Window fabric*: Howe & Bainbridge. *Chair fabric*: Clarence House. *Booth upholstery material*: Naugahyde by Uniroyal. *Custom tables*: Palko Designs & Mfg. *Chairs*: Empire State Chair. *Lighting, metal structure*: Options Lighting. *Custom columns*: Schwerd Mfg. *Marble*: Integrity Tile. *Carpet*: Wunda Weve. *Vinyl tile*: Kentile

WINGS

Location: New York, New York
Seating Capacity: 90
Interior Designer: Geoffrey Hassman
Photographer: Mark Ross

A shaft of pink lighting emanates from the entrance (above). The logo is painted to simulate etching. View of the main dining room on the facing page is seen through petals of giant styrofoam flowers.

Everything is pink—floors, ceiling, walls, fabrics, even the piano—in this popular Soho restaurant located in a former warehouse. The space alloted the designer was the ground floor and basement. By removing a horizontal divider and placing the restaurant on the lower level, the designer was able to double the ceiling height of the installation. To accommodate 90 diners in the narrow 20′ × 60′ main room (overall square footage is approximately 3,000), seating is arranged in three ways: banquettes along one wall, tables-for-two opposite, and twin rows of tables in-between. The main bar is on the entry level, and a secondary bar below it. Coat and rest room facilities are under the balcony.

The arrangement of the space was based on the premise that this was a place for people "to see and be seen." Thus the stairway from the entrance becomes a focal point for guests, in the words of the designer, to "cascade into the dining room." Bright lighting enhances the grand-entrance staging.

The color pink was chosen for its flattering and soothing effect, and 85-feet of neon tube lighting within a grooved ceiling channel adds a note of drama. The name "Wings" was selected by the client for its "melodic and contemporary sound."

General contractor: Vogue Construction. *Carpet:* Wunda Weve. *Upholstery fabrics:* Design Tex. *Neon:* Neon New York. *Lighting:* Lightolier.

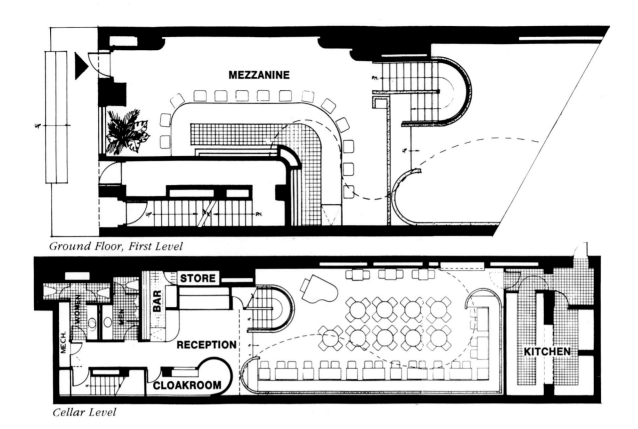

Ground Floor, First Level

Cellar Level

A view of the bar is shown on the facing page. At right is the lower segment of the stairway and below is the main dining room. Eighty-five feet of neon lighting snake across the ceiling. Walls are painted with sparkle-paint, reflective with tiny mica chips air-sprayed into the coating while wet.

ABSOLUTELY GLORIA'S

Location: Cherry Hill, New Jersey
Seating Capacity: 190
Interior Designer: Edwin Bronstein, AIA
Photographer: Russell Abraham

ABSOLUTELY GLORIA'S represents the introduction of a fine, well designed dining facility to a community where few, if any, such restaurants had existed. Thus, architect Edwin Bronstein was faced not only with the expected design problems but also with forming operational solutions. Paramount among the latter was bridging the dichotomy between the site and the owner's perception of what the restaurant should be.

The site is part of a commercial strip development shopping center—incongruous with plans for an upscale dining facility. Added to the incongruity was the problem of how to compete with nearby glitzy establishments without being forced to produce more of the same. Finally, there was another site-related problem. How could people be attracted from the outside while looking in, and then, once inside be presented with other than parking lot views?

Bronstein's theme of a surreal landscape is partially established by an 85-foot-long cloud mural painted behind a built-out colonnade. The focal point, it diverts diners' attention from parking lot views.

48

TRUMPS

Location: Los Angeles, California
Seating Capacity: 122
Interior Designer: Waldo Fernandez
Photographer: Charles White

Originally a gas station and then a to-the-trade showroom for the designer's own furniture collection, the building to accommodate the restaurant required no structural alterations other than the addition of a kitchen and outdoor patio. Its most visible assets, the exposed beams and eight skylights, are part of the original structure.

Since there were to be only two overlapping areas, space planning was easy. Just past the entrance is the bar; beyond is the dining room. Only a low planter partition separates the zones. The overall feeling is quintessential Southern California: light and airy, uncluttered and uncomplicated, monochromatic. Furnishings are all custom, and were subsequently incorporated into the designer's collection, Waldo's Designs. Particularly interesting are the dining and cocktail tables, the bar and the 14″ square floor tiles; they represent results of the designer's experimentation with cast concrete.

General contractor: John Misconie. *Furniture (custom):* Waldo's Designs. *Upholstery fabric:* Vice Versa. *Flooring:* Mission Concrete. *Mirror work:* Custom Glass. *Lighting:* Halo.

Views of the bar and lounge area with a seating capacity of 50. The painting is by California artist Ron David.

The single dining room is separated
from the adjacent lounge by a planter
partition 28" wide, 32" high. Tables are of
cast concrete; chairs have backs and
seats of woven split bamboo.

PEGASUS RESTAURANT

Location: East Rutherford, New Jersey
Seating Capacity: 1500
Interior Designer: Walker/Group, Inc.
Photographer: Mark Ross

The project was a huge one: 96,045 square feet of space encompassing three dining rooms, two bars and pari-mutuel betting facilities on the top floor of the Meadowlands race track grandstand building. Walker/Group, who was responsible for the interior design, space planning and graphics program, worked with The Grad Partnership in a joint venture, the latter firm being responsible for the structural extension of the top level of the building to house the dining facilities.

According to the designers, the movement of people was an important factor in adding excitement to the interior design plan, all of which is heightened in mirror reflections and dramatized by special lighting. As defined by the design team: "It is a people place, a night place."

There are two main dining areas (see plan): one on the west side of the floor, the other on the east. In between are the lounge and bar areas. Betting facilities are behind these spaces. A separate and smaller dining room is located in the south wing and is used for special functions. A glass-enclosed elevator tower was added to provide direct access to the restaurants. In the east and west wing restaurants, rows of ottomans look over a step-down passage to the race track. In the bar sections, facing the betting stations, are wood counters with brass rails. Visible to all in these areas are the electronic monitoring devices which include 184 television sets to give results of the events being held.

Materials were selected both for their ability to take hard abuse and for their appropriateness to different situations—various kinds of marble in heavily trafficked sections; carpeting in the dining/lounge areas; oak veneers for the bars and cabinetry; and mirrors with etched glass to magnify the feeling of motion.

Lighting design was by Gene Stival of Howard Brandston Lighting Design.

Carpet: Kenmore. *Custom tables:* J & B Associates. *Chairs:* Stendig. *Upholstery leather:* Middletown. *Upholstery fabrics:* Dazian's. *Wood cabinetry:* Eckert-Johnson. *Table linens:* James G. Hardy. *China:* Shenango. *Silverware:* Oneida. *Crystal:* Robert Minners.

View from the west end of the restaurant looking over part of the race track's home stretch and to Bergen County.

View above shows the bar in the background as seen from the raised dining platform.
Dining room on the facing page is in the south wing and is used for special functions.

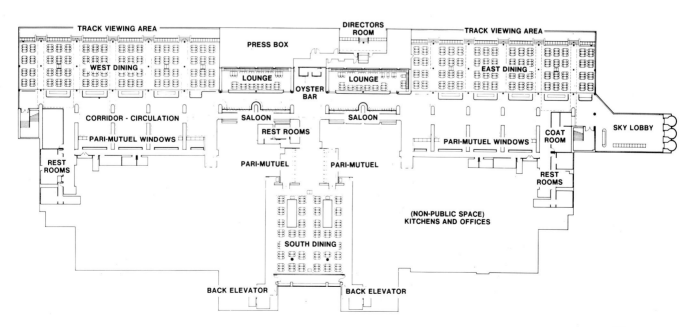

Restaurants with a Theme

Brad Elias on Themes

Mention the term theme restaurant to any sophisticated operator, restaurateur or designer. A disdainful response will most likely follow. The theme restaurant is trite, condescending in tone and passé. In one respect it is. To be successful today, any fine restaurant would eschew obvious overkill with French, Italian or Mexican themes. But, is a theme truly dead? Look at some of the elegant Art Deco styled interiors that are treated more as restorations than as a theatrical settings. Or, take some of the restaurants that convey a sense of elegance with minimal decor. Or, look at those that interpret trendy New Wave culture to attract a particular clientele. These are very much with us, and in a sense represent the so-called theme facilities of today. In each instance, the theme is focused not on mere surface decor, but works as a key element in the marketing concept. This, according to restaurant and hospitality specialist Brad Elias, is what the theme restaurant is all about.

"I look at the theme as a marketing project," he says. "In this respect, every restaurant is a theme restaurant. It has to reach this particular audience; it has to sell this product; it has to feel this way. Who the owner wants to attract influences how the interior will look. It's just like a story line in a movie." Thus, the most important element a client can bring to a designer is a strong concept of target market. What type of personality is he after? Should the restaurant cater to a high or low budgeted meal? Should it aim to attract early diners if, for example, it is situated near a retirement community? Or, will it cater to a late-night stylish crowd? Does a brisk bar business figure into both concept and profit margin? Answers to these questions help form a program's framework. Where there is no predetermined idea, the designer must work to devise one with the client as step one. "When the owner doesn't know what he wants, it makes the designer's job more difficult. It makes it difficult to identify the target market. With today's competitive field, a restaurant can't be all things to all people."

For a designer, establishing a theme is not what is important. What is important is that all the design elements work first: the plan, the circulation flow, lighting, the total ambiance, and appropriateness. Addressing this last factor, Elias compares cities. "In New York and maybe Chicago, one can get away with a lot more than in Los Angeles or Miami. In New York, we crowd them in; people like the excitement. The difference is trying to squeeze four people for dinner at a 36″ tables versus a 42″ table. Or, it can be lining people up on a settee at 24″ wide tables as compared to 30″, with only a foot-and-a-half between them. You can get away with that in New York, Chicago and maybe San Francisco, not in the rest of the country."

The so-called theme, if there is to be one, must be implemented in diluted form. "Today," says Elias, "restaurants make a statement and then they let you alone. Then, it's up to them to provide the food, ambience and a comfortable place to eat. If you're doing a theme restaurant make sure you've got the menu, location, target market and decor all in alignment. And don't underestimate the sophistication of the client."

With the exception of what have become institutions (the Four Seasons and P.J. Clarke's are named), restaurants have surprisingly limited life spans. Five to seven years is the average, with only a limited allowance—maybe three months—for the restaurant to catch on. Naturally, the primary determinant of life cycle is dollar volume. But, Elias also cites two other reasons for limited longevity. In five years, many of the interior elements wear out physically, given the abuse to which they are subjected. Second, styles have changed enough so that the interior may no longer be in vogue. For example, a once fresh color scheme is now the subject of overuse. Or, a theme, particularly one on the cutting edge of the avant-garde, looks tired and dated after a year or two. Unless it keeps changing, this type of trendy treatment may very well bore people after a few visits. Says Elias, "Unless the restaurant has become an institution or *the* classic hangout, it's time for a change." Knowing this, many operators plan from the start to sell their restaurant after three years, capitalizing on its peak popularity—not only for increased profit from the sale, but also for the ease it affords in drawing clientele to the next restaurant. Another alternative, without having to sell and start anew, is to redo surface decor and change the menu to keep pace with changing tastes.

And tastes, including his own says Elias, are changing. "I was an absolute minimalist and my personal taste was the same. But when I do a restaurant now, it's theater. People want to and deserve to be entertained when they pay to go out to eat. The ambience is as important as the food. And people are much more sophisticated now."

While overt themes may be taboo for restaurants seeking an upscaled clientele, they have been adapted by the chain operations. "The national food companies are into food preparation now, and they're looking for themes because they want to reproduce. They're looking for a success formula to compensate for less than brilliant food. This is a whole new category of theme restaurant. The quintessential Third Avenue pub/bar has become the most copied theme in the United States."

BRAD ELIAS is design director/principal of Hochheiser-Elias Design Group, based in New York. Recently completed projects include hotels, food service facilities, a casino and a discotheque.

THE 41st PRECINCT

Location: New York, New York
Seating Capacity: 74 (dining areas); 28 (bar/lounge)
Interior Designer: Hochheiser-Elias Design Group
Photographer: Max Hilaire

A turn-of-the-century police station is the theme of this restaurant on Manhattan's East 41st Street which is aimed at attracting young executives working in the area.

The designers faced two major problems: a modest budget, set at less than $10 a square foot, which ruled out making any major structural changes; and a 25' × 120' tunnel-like space with a monotonous expanse of ceiling. By creating intimate dining islands at different heights (the central dining platform, for example, rises 18″) the effect of being in a long, narrow space is greatly minimized. A lowered ceiling in another area with 40 holophane lights hung from cords relieves the monotony of the ceiling expanse.

The police precinct motif is handled with tongue-in-cheek starting with the exterior logo which is shaped to simulate a policeman's shield. Globe lights marked with the Police Department's initials or precinct number are stationed at corners or partitions. On the walls are theme-related 1890-1900 sepia prints, and bars, suggesting a prison, are used as a divisional device in several areas.

General Contractor: Wellbilt Equipment Corp. *Bar stools, chairs, tables:* L & B Products; *Track lighting:* Halo. *Pole lamps:* Custom Light Styles. *Floor tiles:* Nemo Tile. *Carpet:* Mainline Carpets.

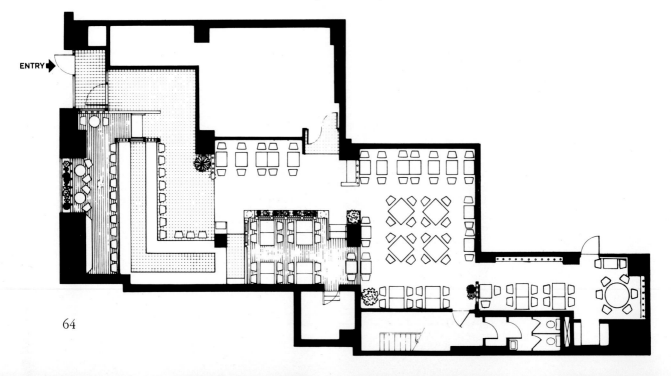

ENTRY ►

64

LALIQUE

Location: Bal Harbour, Florida
Seating Capacity: 122 (dining); 23 (lounge)
Interior Designer: Creative Environs
Photographer: Dan Forer

Entrance to the restaurant is shown above with an original glass piece by René Lalique mounted on a cylindrical pedestal. View of the main dining room is on the facing page.

One of the more popular themes in current restaurant design is Art Deco and an excellent example of combining this romantic style of the 20's with contemporary decor is LALIQUE, a Florida restaurant named for René Lalique, the well-known French Art Nouveau jeweler and glass designer. In addition to its eye appeal, Art Deco design was an appropriate theme for the restaurant which is located in the midst of some of the finest examples of Art Deco buildings in the country.

Soft, rounded forms are used throughout the restaurant, and all the major design elements—the channel-quilted banquettes, love-seats and chairs, free-standing columns and interior partitions—have gentle, rounded contours. Even the wall sconces, which are based on a classic Art Deco design, taper gently to form a trumpet shape. The color palette is equally restrained—rich hues of gray, teal blue and burgundy, contrasted with pink table linens. The result is a restaurant interior which is soft, subdued and invitingly gracious.

Carpet: Durkan. *Dining chairs:* Swaim Originals; Shelby Williams. *Lighting fixtures:* Metropolitan Lighting; Lite-Makers. *Decorative mirror:* Farallon Studios. *Etched glass murals:* Joan of Art.

Rounded and contoured furniture and architectural elements blend well with the Art Deco motifs. An etched glass mural depicting a pair of cranes forms the focal point in this area of the restaurant.

LE TRAIN BLEU

Location: New York, New York
Seating Capacity: 67
Interior Designer: Fred Palatinus
Photographer: Jaime Ardiles-Arce

This restaurant, which opened on the sixth floor of Bloomingdale's in 1979, takes its name and design theme from the famous Le Train Bleu which ran between Paris and the Riviera in the 20's. Authenticity is the key-note, for although the restaurant is not an exact replica of the original train, the design-er based much of his design on research about trains in order to get the true height of a railroad car, determine what the windows were like and ascertain the modulation of the space. The result is a composite of what ele-gant railway dining cars looked like in the 20's. The only major change was expansion of the width of the space from the normal 10′ to 14′ in order to provide greater aisle and seat-ing area. Green, which was a typical color of the period, appears in the velvet seat uphol-stery and in a quilted version on the walls and ceiling. Final touches of authenticity are brass luggage racks above each table for storage of packages.

Fabrication of woodwork and the train shell: Jaff Brothers. *Metalwork:* Norris Metals. *Interior carpet:* Couristan. *Lighting fixtures:* Greene Bros. *Chairs and table bases:* Chairmasters. *Velvet fabric:* Stroheim & Romann.

70

CAPRICCIO ITALIANO

Location: Atlantic City, New Jersey
Seating Capacity: 130
Interior Designer: Valerian Rybar
Photographer: Jaime Ardiles-Arce

Part of the Resorts International casino complex, CAPRICCIO ITALIANO presented designer Valerian Rybar with "a Palladian ballroom-sized area." It was these grand proportions that determined the restaurant's design theme—one of old-world elegance. Through color, a series of eight murals commissioned to recall Tiepolo paintings, and added architectural detailing, Rybar created a setting reminiscent of a chamber in an Italian palazzo. Particularly important were the detail elements—mouldings, doorway arches and shaped cutouts to frame the paintings. These not only lend authenticity to the motif but also add definition and a sense of scale to what might otherwise be an overwhelming expanse.

There are two dining rooms, each with the same tone and similar furnishing elements. The smaller room offers cocktail in addition to dining service, and overlooks Atlantic City's boardwalk and the sea. Seating is for parties of two or four; the main dining room is primarily for groups of six or more.

Carpet: Brintons. *Millwork (custom):* Midhattan Woodworking. *Lighting:* Gem Monogram & Cut Glass Corp. *Banquettes:* Chairmasters. *Chairs, bar stools:* Shelby Williams. *Upholstery fabric:* Schumacher. *Wall coverings:* Schumacher; Wolf Gordon.

Two views of the main dining room. The series of columns supporting arched spandrels near the windows is one of the few features retained from the original structure.
Two service stations at either end of the room's center are joined by an island of alcove seating to create a subtle traffic flow pattern and prevent the room from being a sea of tables.

RESTAURANT JONATHAN

Location: New Orleans, Louisiana
Seating Capacity: 150
Interior Designer: Jack Cosner
Photographer: Jaime Ardiles-Arce

Dominating the entrance foyer is Dennis Abbé's canvas mural of aquatic life and maitre d's stand which is finished with black lacquer, gold leaf and eggshell. The ceiling, with its ziggurat lightwell, is covered with gold foil squares that have been given a tortoise treatment. The bronze lamp and vase are originals.

RESTAURANT JONATHAN is a near-perfect example of an Art Deco interpretation, that although implemented in 1977, looks anything but trite today. The main reason is co-owner/architect/designer Jack Cosner's approach to the theme. For he conjoined and renovated two abandoned townhouses to create a virtual Art Deco museum. "At first," he says, "I planned to base the motif on Hollywood Deco. When I discovered that original material was available, I decided to design an authentic Deco installation rather than a stage set. Jonathan is authentic because it's concerned with architectural elements, spatial flow and what was really used then, as opposed to present conceptions of the period."

Preliminary structural renovation centered on establishing a flow among the three floors, with patios and terraces providing supplementary visual linkage. Then, the space was divided to accommodate six dining/lounge facilities each with a distinct character and color palette. On the first floor are the Night and Day lounge with oxblood/black/gold coloration and the salmon and gray toned Paradise room. Main dining rooms, called Erté and Icart, are on the second floor and characterized by a dark blue/silver palette. Two private dining rooms—one is silver and blue, and other in bold Mardi Gras colors—occupy the third level. Kitchen and support systems are on the first floor.

What truly make this interior are the art, objects and attention to detail. Aside from original works, most extraordinary are Dennis Abbés commissioned murals and glass pieces, the major one a panel rising two stories from the lounge through the ceiling into the Icart dining room. Detail work includes crown moldings cast from originals at Manhattan's Roxy Theater, special door frames, and judicious use of the ziggurat deco signature. In nine-and-a-half months, Cosner recreated an era in New Orleans.

Floor tile: American Olean. *Lighting fixtures:* Lightolier; Camer; A & G Machinery Co. *Dining tables (custom bar stools):* L&B Manufacturing. *Dining chairs:* Fanta. *Upholstery vinyl:* Naugahyde by Uniroyal. *Carpet:* Magee. *Cocktail tables:* Gampel-Stoll. *Lounge chairs:* Jansko. *Banquettes* (custom): Orleans Cabinet Works.

The silver and blue Erté dining room is on the second floor and opens onto a
balcony. The wall covering on the far wall is made from half-rounds and wood lathes.
The figure in the foreground is a signed French bronze; the sconces
(circa 1928) are from part of the Smithsonian Institution that has been demolished.

The salmon and blue-gray color palette of the Paradise room makes this the most
tranquil dining area. To the rear is the glass work that separates this from the
Night and Day Lounge. Art Deco accents include an original figurine of silver washed
copper on an etched glass globe and mirrored detailing on the custom banquettes.

MAX'

Location: Atlanta, Georgia
Seating Capacity: 222
Interior Designer: Donghia-Martin
Photographer: Jaime Ardiles-Arce

View of the entrance looking towards the bar whose up-front location helps draw potential patrons into the restaurant. The flooring is of oak as are the wide handrails accented with polished brass detailing.

"Chic western" was the design motif selected for Max' restaurant, an independently owned facility within Atlanta's Omni hotel. Although the theme was executed by Angelo Donghia and Robert Martin, credit for the project is shared by a triumverate including owner Max Schnallinger and architects Jova Daniels Busby as well as the interior designers.

True, the designers did use plenty of the obvious elements associated with the theme. Yet the design was also predicated on factors more complex than mere visuals. First, there were decisions relating to site selection and general operating procedures, these mainly the client's concern. The restaurant is located on a central promenade one level above the ice rink, and has high visibility within the hotel complex. This visibility, coupled with the up-front location of the bar, helps to entice passers-by, hotel guests, local Atlantans and spectators from the neighboring sports coliseum, all viewed as potential patrons.

Another design decision centered on space planning for the 7,250-square-foot public space. There are three dining areas plus a lounge; divisions were effected only by level changes and what the designers term "knee walls" (about 30" high), leaving open views of the entire restaurant from any point. Although there is an undisputed unity of tone achieved through materials and accessories, each dining area does differ slightly from the others to avoid an institutional look. Variances come from a diversity of seating and from lighting changes. There is track lighting in the lounge and dining area B, and a combination of track and suspended fixtures in dining area A (see plan). In dining area C, the largest and most formal, there are three central chandeliers and a suspended fixture over each table. James Nuckolls was responsible for the lighting design.

General contractor: Ira. H. Hardin Co. *Sisal floor covering:* Ernest Treganowan. *Carpet wall covering:* Patterson, Flynn & Martin. *Dining chairs:* Terra Furniture. *Dining tables:* L&B Products (bases); Charles Lindlom (marble tops). *Banquettes:* Interior Crafts. *Upholstery fabrics:* Vice Versa. *Lighting:* Lighting Associates.

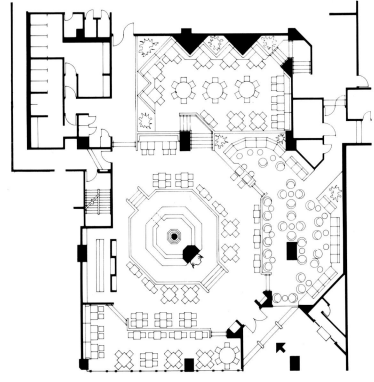

Visible from the lounge are the bar and one of the dining rooms. Emphasizing the large scale of the octagonal shaped bar is a wood railing canopy whose column supports incorporate glass storage.

THE GOLDEN DRAGON

Location: Knoxville, Tennessee
Seating Capacity: 75-90
Interior Designer: Interior Associates, Inc.
Photographer: Larry Taylor, Format Photography

The space: an existing Knoxville store, 121' long and 23' wide. The assignment: create a Chinese restaurant with a full service kitchen. The budget: less than $20,000.

In carrying out the program, the designers avoided the usual hackneyed Oriental trappings and created a restaurant with a fresh interpretation of Chinese colorings and symbols.

A curvilinear theme is introduced in painted sheet metal at the entryway which spells out the name of the restaurant in both English and Chinese. The same shape is repeated inside in illuminated canvas room dividers reminiscent of festive Chinese paper lanterns. A central row of tables leads the eye to a brilliant red point formed by the angle of the service bar which juts into the dining area. This device introduces a color contrast that marks the transition from the green dining area to the red service areas.

The seating arrangement places bench seating at tables for two down each outside wall, and tables for four, placed on the diagonal, down the center of the room. A small alcove behind the reception area accommodates a grouping of five tables for four. A white metal grid system with track lighting runs diagonally through the restaurant under the existing ceiling which has been "blacked out" with paint.

Chairs: Falcon. *Laminate surfaces of custom tables:* Formica. *Upholstery:* Carnegie. *Track lighting:* Lightolier. *Carpet:* Stratton. *Ceiling grid:* Armstrong.

THE PRINCESS

Location: Century City, California
Seating Capacity: 124
Architects: Arechaederra, Hong & Treiman
Interior Designer: Hirsch/Bedner Associates
Photographer: Charles White

Its predecessor was a Mexican restaurant replete with crude woodwork and cheap Spanish tile. The program: create a high-caliber restaurant within an Italian villa-like setting. It was the first attempt by Princess Cruise Lines, known for culinary excellence on its cruise ships, to establish a land-based restaurant.

Fortunately, the existing architecture was well suited to its new purpose with a two-story skylit central atrium and dramatic arches. What was needed was extensive cosmetic surgery to remove the remnants of its predecessors, to enlarge doorways and create windows. The result was a transformation into an interior with the design and mood of a Mediterranean villa. Interior walls were painted and textured white and accented with beige and pastel tones. Classical fresco-like decoration was added. Marble panels replaced the Spanish tile, and large expanses of glass were added to three of the exterior walls so that every room now overlooks a landscaped garden.

James Northcutt was the project interior designer; John Watson was lighting designer.

Banquettes and dining chairs: Stewart Collection. *Upholstery fabrics:* Maharam; Architex. *Carpet:* Victoria. *Hanging lanterns:* Boyd.

CLYDE'S AT TYSONS CORNER

Location: Tysons Corner, Virginia
Seating Capacity: 400
Architect/Interior Designer: John Richards Andrews
Photographer: Mark Ross

View of exterior is shown above. The Palm Terrace, seen on the facing page, is a garden room with natural light filtering through the 27' high glass roof.

Although the theme is not specifically Art Nouveau or Art Deco, this 9,360 square foot restaurant features numerous original bronzes in those styles intermingled with a vast assortment of other decorative objects including stained glass, paintings and posters. The fourth in a series of food facilities by the same owners, the newer addition differs considerably from its predecessors, which are primarily bars where food is incidental, by concentrating on fine fare in an elegant setting. It is located in a stylish structure especially designed to house it. The overall effect of the exterior, according to the architect, is a tongue-in-cheek interpretation of a 1920's roadhouse with a touch of Grecian temple.

The interior space, although divided into specific dining and bar areas, has no fixed partitions. The various areas flow into a single entity, unified through coloration and a predominant ceiling height of 9'4". The openness obviously invites "people watching", but there are numerous other sights to please the eye—a 75'-long mural by Washington artist William Woodward; intricate woodwork of two large bars; stained glass corner windows; carved glass panels; 40 lamp shades by a Vermont glass sculptor; and a veritable superabundance of artworks and rare objects, each a display piece in its own right yet completely integrated into the overall interior plan.

Custom seating, banquettes, bar and bar stools: Artcraft Woodworking. *Chairs:* Thonet (Palm Terrace); Peter Danko (Cafe, Grill). *Leather on chairs:* Lackawanna. *Table linens:* J. G. Hardy. *Flatware:* Oneida. *China:* Syracuse.

The Cafe with its romantic statuary, stained glass window wall and original Art Nouveau posters. This area is an informal dining facility serviced by a separate kitchen.

92

THE BIG FOUR

Location: San Francisco, California
Seating Capacity: 70
Interior Designer: Anthony Hail
Photographer: William A. Porter

The theme in this elegant restaurant evokes the feeling of an Edwardian man's club and recalls San Francisco's past by referring to the city's four founding tycoons—Collis Huntington, Mark Hopkins, Leland Stanford and Charles Crocker. It achieves this subtly without bogging down in literal reproduction.

The look of a man's club is achieved with a background that incorporates walnut paneling, carved cornices and Ionic columns. But there is none of the heaviness usually associated with this type of interior, and the overall space is brightened with lighting and an abundant use of clear, stained, mirrored, carved, etched and beveled glass.

Although the names of San Francisco's "big four" are etched into the glass tops of the cocktail lounge tables, other references to them are suggestive rather than literal and can be seen in posters, photographs and memorabilia of early California.

Unity is achieved throughout (in addition to the dining room proper there is a bar and cocktail lounge and a private dining room for 40) by repetition of the basic furnishings—green-covered open armchairs and banquettes and brass table lamps.

General contractor: George Drury. *Carpet:* Milliken. *Chairs:* Interior Crafts. *Upholstery:* Naugahyde by Uniroyal. *Bar stools:* Buzan Co. *Dining room light fixtures:* Roundtree. *Horn sconces:* Chapman.

Shown at right is the inner lobby of the restaurant with period paneling and beveled glass. On the facing page: the main dining room as seen reflected in carved mirror panels reiterating the sources of the fortunes of San Francisco's "big four" for whom the restaurant was named.

94

At left is the reception room which is entered from the street via a short flight of stairs. At the top of the opposite page, an overall view of the main dining room.

Left and opposite page: the cocktail lounge and bar. The glass tops of the tables in the lounge are etched underneath with the names of the "big four". Behind the bar is a variety of framed memorabilia of early California.

SLOTNICK'S DAUGHTER

Location: New York, New York
Seating Capacity: 28
Interior Designer: Interior Concepts
Photographer: Jaime Ardiles-Arce

Located in Manhattan's Citicorp building, this compact 930-square-foot facility is a fast-food restaurant, a retail shop for coffee and tea, and a take-out food service all rolled into one. Yet it displays none of the stereotypes usually associated with such installations. Instead, this is an extraordinarily well-planned project where three distinct function areas are joined in a strong architectural entity.

Starting with raw space, the designers partitioned it into almost equal thirds to accommodate each separate yet related function. Since the food for the limited menu is not actually cooked, but only assembled on-site, there was no need for a proper kitchen; only a dishwashing area was allocated. Then, dining tables were located in the rear of the space, with banquette seating built into the end wall. The food preparation and service counter were located to the left of the entry; the coffee and tea sales counter to the right.

The designers selected a single element, a two-inch-square ceramic tile, to form both the architectural shell and some of the furnishings. It provides unity to the three zones within the space, covering floor, walls and the stepped service counter in the sales sector. Elsewhere, complementary materials of glass, mirror and polished stainless steel were deployed, and to counteract their austerity, plum and green upholstery fabrics were chosen. Lighting is from incandescent sources in recessed fixtures. Supplementary spotlights highlight the food display and decorative objects in niches along the wall in the sales area.

General contractor: Herbert Construction. *Tile:* American Olean. *Tables:* L&B Products. *Chairs:* Stendig. *Upholstery fabrics:* Arc-Com. *Custom cabinetry:* Mandas & Orr. *Lighting:* Lightolier.

E.A.T.

Location: Horseheads, New York
Seating Capacity: 100
Interior Designer: Stockman & Manners Associates
Photographer: George Cserna

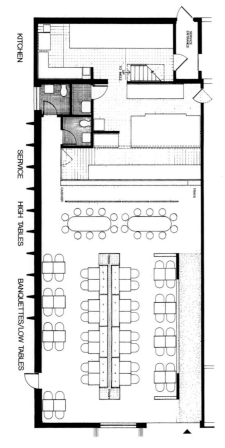

For this fast-food facility located in a shopping mall in upstate New York, Judith Stockman and Lee Manners based their design solution in direct response to the target market and competition. This cafeteria-style eatery had to appeal to a broad group of shoppers, mall employees, businessmen and families. Given its location, it had to respect the prospective clientele's rather limited exposure to sophisticated design. And, it had to encourage a rapid turnover.

The solution, according to the designers, is "a crisp environment," warmed by natural materials and such familiar elements as beaded oak strip detailing, a pressed tin ceiling, oak flooring, white ceramic tile, cocoa mat, and glass lighting shades.

Within the space, Stockman & Manners created three seating options: stand-up-tables for quick meals located closest to the service counter, a central banquette, or tables lining the walls. Tables are two deuces joined together so they may be used for parties of two or four. Located at both ends of the central banquette are built-in trash receptacles that must be passed when the customer exits.

Rather than the uniform lighting that is customary in this type of installation, the solution here provides a variety of light levels. A recessed cove around the perimeter is fitted with G-lamps that reflect light off the oak walls, and the cove continues outside the restaurant to the mall. Over the service counter are pendant fixtures throwing pools of light.

The artwork, also an unusual touch for a cafeteria, holds great appeal for local residents. A series of photographs of local scenes was selected by the designers in collaboration with the client.

General contractor: Streeter Associates. *Ceiling:* Barney Barnium Shanker Steel Co. *Chairs:* Thonet. *Tables:* L&B Products. *Lighting fixtures:* Harry Gitlin; Keene Lighting. *Tile:* American Olean. *Upholstery canvas and banner material:* John Boyle. *Cocoa matting:* Allied Mat and Matting. *Banquette upholstery:* Foam-Tex.

DETROIT COFFEE HOUSE

Location: Detroit International Airport, Michigan
Seating Capacity: 100
Interior Designer: Denis Allemand & Associates Design
Photographer: Alexandre Georges

The client was Host International Corporation of Santa Monica, said to be the world's largest restaurant facility operator. Having done much of their previous work, the designer was thoroughly familiar with the operation and the firm's requirements. Space plans of all Host restaurants are related, but the design treatment depends on the location.

The Detroit facility is situated in a newly constructed building designed by Louis Redstone Associates. The design approach was to integrate the coffee shop with its architectural shell and to establish an identity without in any way clashing with the building. Consequently, concrete walls and columns are left exposed; a vertically striped wall covering above the serving line echoes the pattern of a ribbed concrete wall; and the large-scale identification signage is recessed into the ceiling slab. Lighting is ceiling mounted and recessed with concealed wall washers to accent framed graphics and hanging tapestries.

Floor tile: Architectural Ceramic Surfaces. *Chairs*: F. W. Lombard. *Tables, banquettes, fixtures*: Stainless Equipment Mfg. Co. *Vinyl upholstery*: Naugahyde by Uniroyal. *Table laminate*: Nevamar. *Wall covering*: Genon by General Tire. *Tapestries*: Regal Rugs.

DOBB'S HOUSE

Location: Miami International Airport, Florida
Seating Capacity: 48
Interior Designer: Dennis Jenkins Associates
Photographer: Dan Forer

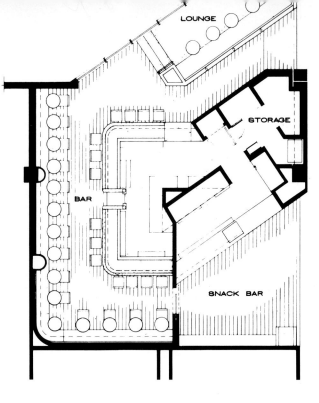

THE DOBB'S HOUSE snack bar and lounge is a welcome change from the thousands of fast-food services that fill the nation's airports. As designed by Barbara Magruder of Dennis Jenkins Associates in collaboration with Milton C. Harry Associates, Architects, this eye-catching project fits several functional requirements within a limited 1048-square-foot area.

Originally smaller, DOBB'S HOUSE was enlarged with a greenhouse extension along a runway's edge; the addition provided room for a small sunken lounge to supplement the bar/lounge and snack bar. Identical furnishings and materials were used to unify the sectors: oak for flooring, furniture and woodworking; deep green vinyl for upholstery; mirror-finished aluminum slats for the ceiling. Additional elements, whimsical in nature, add character to the space: a dome-shaped canopy over the bar, colorful kites, arched lighting poles.

From an operational view, one of the most interesting aspects of the restaurant is the remote liquor delivery system, specially adapted by the manufacturer and designer. Bottles are stored in custom-built wall cabinets, and the liquor, whose flow is forced by gravitational pull, travels through a system of tubes concealed in the columns and ceiling to dispensers behind the bar. This system, according to the designer, "has changed the look and function of the conventional snack bar, freeing the floor plan and allowing more seating with less clutter for this fast-paced service operation."

Chairs and bar stools: Hank Loewenstein. *Upholstery vinyls:* Wolf Gordon; Naugahyde by Uniroyal. *Tables:* L&B Products; Eckes Assoc. *Oak flooring:* Endurance Floor. *Lighting:* Benjamin Lighting. *Cabinetry:* Atlantic Millwork; Grove Woodworks. *Metal work:* Tropex Corp. *Canopy:* Thomas Awnings. *Greenhouse:* Lord & Burnham. *Ceiling:* Willard Ceiling Systems. *Liquor system:* Benner Equipment.

CECI'S RESTAURANT

Location: New York, New York
Seating Capacity: 95
Interior Designer: Nicholas A. Calder
Photographer: Victoria Lefcourt

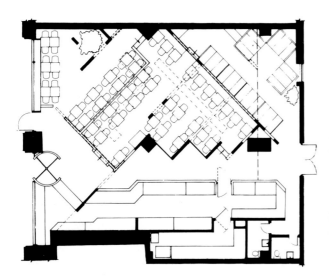

Located in a former Zum-Zum branch, CECI's is aimed at up-and-coming executives in the area looking for good food in a pleasant setting. The 2,200-square-foot space was completely gutted and visually divided into three sections: a front area near the window, the main segment in the center, and a more intimate area in the rear. Defining the three areas, but not completely closing them off, are 36″ to 48″ partitions with arched cut-outs. The central area is also elevated 14″. Suspended soffits further reinforce the illusion of architectural definition. The kitchen is left exposed to cast attention on meal preparation.

Colored neon tubes add shimmering tones to the glossy white surfaces. Supplementary lighting fixtures consist of bulbs with brushed aluminum under glass. Chairs, found in a Bowery supply house, were lacquered and angled at back-rests to suggest Art Deco styling, and table tops are set on soldered-together steel shafts. Banquettes are used in the rear section only.

Upholstery fabrics: Etalage; Craig. *Lighting design and fixtures:* Steven Liting & Design. *Neon:* West Side Neon.

CAFE FLEDERMAUS

Location: New York, New York
Seating Capacity: 30
Interior Designer: Lugrin/Dundes Design
Photographer: Elliot Fine

CAFE FLEDERMAUS in downtown Manhattan represents a new genre of restaurants. It is an elegant stand-up coffee/wine/champagne bar with self-service canapes, fashioned somewhat after Milan's Cova on Via Montenapoleone.

The 600-square-foot space, located in a landmark building, is designed as a prototype for potential future projects. It is a symbolic space where signature elements were carefully selected to bear intimations of Hoffman, Wagner, Klimt and the Austrian Secessionists. Determing this prototypical formula was the most challenging aspect of the project. What Jean Lugrin and Kate Dundes came up with were: black and white marble tile flooring; a black marble counter circling the perimeter; and a scored laminate wall treatment based on eight-inch-wide panels mounted with black anodized channel reveals between them. A hand-painted canvas frieze, also part of the prototypical package, lends color to an otherwise austere interior.

A second graphic element, also the work of the designers, is a pragmatic solution to an operational problem as well as an aesthetic element. How could customers carry their canapes to the counter or tables, or take them home? The solution: boxes that are pulled out from wall storage where they also form an abstract black and white pattern.

The project, completed in eight weeks, also entailed design of the preparatory space, consciously located in full-view from the public sector; the kitchen; offices and a mechanical system.

General contractor: John La Barco of Jamco Industries. *Marble flooring:* T&A Anzovino. *Laminate:* Formica. *Bar stools:* All State Upholstery & Manufacturing. *Lighting fixtures, table bases, brass work (all custom):* Model Brass & Bronze Corporation. *Display cases:* Federal; Traulsen.

PATISSERIE LANCIANI

Location: New York, New York
Seating Capacity: 30
Interior Designer: Kevin Walz
Photographer: Peter Vitale

Originally, up-front retail space for PATISSERIE LANCIANI consisted of a counter and three stools in an area of just 225 square feet. As the shop's popularity grew in its West Greenwich Village neighborhood, and as the client's recently started wholesale business became more lucrative, Patisserie Lanciani had to expand its operation. When the adjacent building became available, Kevin Walz was commissioned to conjoin the two spaces. One proviso of the project was the inclusion of a cafe. As the first true public space, it was to reflect the firm's growing success.

This new up-front cafe encompasses 1,000 square feet and represents about one-fourth the area of the combined sites; most of the rest is devoted to kitchen facilities. In theme, the cafe is based on the seemingly disparate characteristics of the American diner and the Viennese cafe. The diner sensibility, with its accent on comfort and a boisterous nature, was chosen because it guaranteed appeal to the projected clientele. To make the association, Walz used materials and elements that held quintessential American references: simple tables and chairs; tile flooring; the pervasive use of glass block to act as a screening device between the retail area and kitchen behind, as well as partitions to separate waiting customers from those already seated. The European influence, according to the designer, comes mainly from the color palette: the glossy pale lavender of walls (detailed with a hospital bumper strip 24" from the floor to minimize scuffing from chairs); the slight green tint of the glass block; the black lacquer of the chairs.

Illumination comes from incandescent low-heat sources (a consideration when dealing with pastries) with the light diffused through baffles of milky acrylic. The reflector sides of these sources have an iridescent metal finish that serves to reflect prisms on the ceiling.

Floor tile: American Olean. *Chairs:* Falcon. *Tables:* L&B Products. *Lighting:* Harry Gitlin. *Baffles:* Premier Plastics. *Glass block:* PPG. *Table service:* Professional Kitchen. *Refrigeration cabinetry:* C. Schmidt Company.

Patisserie Lanciani

FRANKS FOR THE MEMORY

Location: Vancouver, Canada
Interior Designer: Shelly Mirich Designs
Photographer: Gary Otte

This 1,000-square-foot hot dog stand with its unlikely name is located in a restored waterfront building that functions as a terminal for the city's transit system. This means that the building, always crowded with commuters, should offer great potential for retail sales—provided the product is right and the shop design arresting.

In planning this small facility within the architecturally grand space, Mirish first considered two alternatives. He could continue the architectural detail of the concourse through the leased space. Or, he could paint the stand the same colors as its background and use unobtrusive fixturing. Either solution would have effectively melded the hot dog stand with its site. But Mirich rejected both plans and went in the opposite direction. His restaurant is designed to stand out.

Franks for the Memory is created to simulate the fairground and sporting event ambiences where hot dogs are usually the staple bill of fare. Some ingenious design elements establish the association. Self-executed murals, behind a chain link fence for crowd control, provide a background depiction of enthusiastic fans. A bay of lockers conceals restaurant equipment; the wall-hung menu resembles a scoreboard; the floor covering is synthetic turf; background sounds are recordings of the noises customarily associated with these events. To impart further authenticity, Mirich included two life-size mannequins.

All construction and props (custom): Mirich Developments. *Floor covering:* Dandy Lawn by Amoco Fabrics. *Lighting fixtures:* Lightolier. *Plastic laminates:* Formica.

114

FRANKS FOR THE MEMORY

NEW YORK DELICATESSEN

Location: New York, New York
Seating Capacity: 300
Interior Designer: Hochheiser-Elias
    Design Group
Photographer: Peter Paige

For many years it was a Horn & Hardart Automat on Manhattan's West 57th Street. It subsequently underwent several unfortunate "renovations" and served most recently as a bookshop. Its latest and total transformation is the NEW YORK DELICATESSEN restaurant in a setting which the designer Brad Elias describes as "Hollywood Deco, reminiscent of a Busby Berkley movie set with a touch of Radio City Music Hall."

The main challenge was how to soften and humanize the huge, cavernous space and how to unify the disjointed balcony and main floor expanses, measuring 3,000 and 5,500 square feet respectively. This was achieved by restructuring the seating layout into a series of elevations, each forming a separate island for dining. There are eight such zones in all: a front segment rising 21″ above floor level; two walkway-traversed enclaves, each raised 15″ in the center; a fourth dining area, 36″ high along the wall opposite the delicatessen counter; the balcony which provides seating for 100 in an L-shaped space; a more secluded dining space directly under the balcony; a table for six near the stairs; and, a barrier-free seating space for twelve with special furniture and a privacy screen for the handicapped.

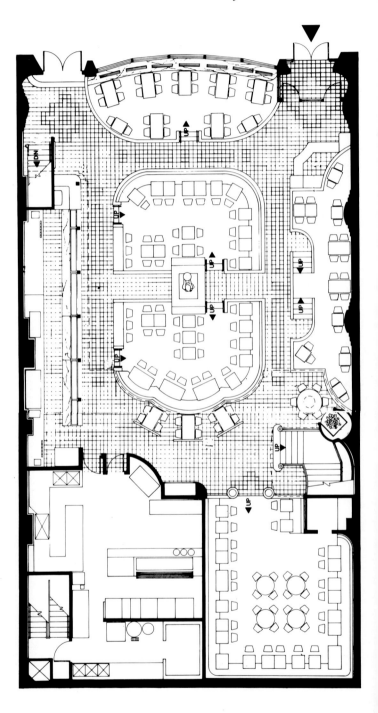

Many of the existing architectural and decorative elements of the original space were retained or adapted for re-use: hand-cast ceramic wainscots, full-height plaster pilasters, decorative carvings, a stair railing with cast glass inserts, and a still-working wall clock. New ingredients, all evoking a feeling of the dominant Deco styling of the entire building, include custom murals based on a 1927 magazine illustration; illuminated glass medallions; etched mirrorwork; and patterned floor tiles.

To help tame the deplorable acoustics, the designer specified heavy-weight carpeting and noise-absorbent tiles in the coffers between plaster beams, and divided the space with staggered multi-height partitions. The disparate seating levels also influenced the choice of lighting. The solution involved fixtures with quartz lamps to illuminate the full-height areas, and incandescent lamps for lower sections. In the back room and under steps, recessed lights are used. The food service area is lit with fluorescents shielded behind gold parabolic lenses, whereas directly over the counters, miniature low-voltage fixtures create an optical blending into the softer lighting of the dining space. All lights are on dimmers, and nowhere does one encounter the harsh glare often associated with delicatessens. Christopher Harms served as lighting consultant.

The food dispensing operation is given focal prominence with marble service counters and display dishes backed by gleaming tiles. Waiters' stations, on the other hand, are out of sight. Each level has its own kitchen.

General contractor: Wellbilt Equipment Corp. *Custom carpet:* Durkan Enterprises. *Recessed and architectural lighting:* Lightlab. *Chairs, tables:* Empire State Chair. *Custom case pieces, banquettes:* Art Fabricators. *Seating covers:* Naugahyde by Uniroyal. *Wall coverings:* Gilford; I.D. International. *Ceramic floor tiles:* Innovative Tile Distributors. *Acoustical ceiling tiles:* U.S. Gypsum.

THE MANSION ON TURTLE CREEK

Location: Dallas, Texas
Seating Capacity: 64 (main dining room)
Interior Designer: Hirsch/Bedner & Associates
Photographer: Jaime Ardiles-Arce

The original entrance to the mansion now leads to the restaurant as seen on the facing page. The walls are painted to resemble stonework; the marble floor was existing.

When Rosewood Hotels decided to erect a deluxe hotel in Dallas, the site selected was the fashionable residential area called Turtle Creek, and the genesis of the project was a 1925 mansion once used as the residence of Shepherd King. A nine-story hotel was built, and the mansion, which offered 10,000 square feet of space on three levels, was converted into a lavish restaurant complex consisting of a main dining room, enclosed terrace room, cocktail lounge, bar, a ballroom and several private dining spaces.

The mansion had undergone several phases of renovation going back to the 40's when it was converted into offices. The starting point in the new conversion was to put the house back to what it had originally been and then to decide what was worth keeping.

The outstanding room was the original dining room with an elaborate ceiling design consisting of 2,400 separate pieces of enameled and inlaid wood. Six workmen spent eight weeks in restoring it. This subsequently became the main dining room of the restaurant. In other areas, new architectural elements had to be added. In the bar the space was completely gutted and a new beamed ceiling added. In areas where there were no architectural details of any consequence, artists were hired to create them.

In the two-story entrance foyer to the restaurant, for example, walls are painted to resemble stone and the curved arches are emphasized with painted textures. The result, here and throughout the complex, is a clever mixture of *trompe l'oeil* and the real thing, a skillful blending of old and new.

James Northcutt was the project interior designer.

General contractor: Linbeck Construction Co. *Tables, banquettes in main dining room:* Cedarquist. *Chairs:* Shelby Williams. *Carpet:* Feltex. *Upholstery fabrics:* Contex, Pacific Hide, Stroheim & Romann. *Lamps:* Donghia. *Table linens:* Baker. *China:* Shenago. *Flatware:* Oneida.

In the main dining room, the elaborate inlaid wood ceiling was carefully restored, the back wall mirrored to dramatize the fireplace which is actually plaster but has been painted to resemble carved limestone; walls are upholstered with fabric, and the artwork is of museum quality. The restaurant is managed by the "21" Club of New York.

The space now encompassing the bar (above) was completely gutted and beams added to the ceiling. Walls here and in the adjoining lounge (right) are upholstered in dark green velvet and decorated with equestrian paints and hunt trophies. The floor is the original marble in a parquetry pattern.

LA TOUR RESTAURANT

Location: Chicago, Illinois
Seating Capacity: 186
Interior Designer: Hirsch/Bedner & Associates
Photographer: Jaime Ardiles-Arce

As part of a complete renovation of the Park Hyatt Hotel on Chicago's Water Tower Place, it was decided to extend the building onto Michigan Avenue to provide 700 square feet of space for a restaurant. The result: LA TOUR, which like the rest of the renewed hotel spaces, emphasizes fine materials and a feeling of luxury.

The effect, especially in the daytime, is that of being in a greenhouse with floor-to-ceiling expanses of glass. Flooring is polished marble flagstone with cement grouting, accented with custom area rugs designed by Katt Hirsch (the designer's daughter). Artworks include Rousseau-like murals painted by Richard Gabriel Chass.

A nighttime view of the restaurant is shown on the facing page. Other areas include lounge seating for after-dinner drinks, and a cocktail lounge with a grand piano.

Restaurant chairs: Shelby Williams. *Upholstery fabric*: Contex. *Flooring*: Natural Stone & Marble. *Custom area rugs*: Tai Ping. *Lounge seating, bar stools*: du Rovan. *Banquettes*: Equipment Mfg.

THE COPLEY PLAZA RESTAURANTS

Location: Boston, Massachusetts
Seating Capacity: 66 (Cafe Plaza)
Interior Designer: Anita Tremain
Photographer: Jaime Ardiles-Arce

Shown on the facing page is a view of the hotel's elegant Cafe Plaza. The draperies were refashioned from those formerly used in the ballroom.

When, in the late 70's, a program was undertaken to restore the venerable Copley-Plaza to its "former elegance," the restaurants were a major part of the overall renovation. In some spaces—the new Cafe Plaza, shown on the facing page, for example—complete remodeling was required; others, such as the famous Copley's Bar, shown on the following spread, were architecturally unchanged.

The Cafe Plaza is the most elegant of the hotel's several dining rooms, and its transformation was the most drastic, requiring the services of skilled craftsmen to create faux bois treatments for the lower sections of the walls, for example, to match the upper real wood portions. The 30-foot high vaulted ceiling in the room was transformed by the same artisans into a cameo-effect canopy through painting, shading and glazing. The drapery fabrics were salvaged from the ballroom and refashioned for use here into an elegantly swagged window treatment. The Waterford crystal chandelier was existing but had to be dismantled and cleaned.

In Copley's Bar, the authentic Edwardian flavor of the room was enhanced by varied painting techniques, among them faux bois and tortoise shell finishes for the central structure; gold leafing and glazing on the ceiling. On the surrounding mirrors are oil portraits of local personalities, executed in the fashion of the early 1900's by artist Ted Seth Jacobs. Old lighting fixtures include sconces from a defunct Schrafft's.

A series of three dining rooms is located off the bar (total seating capacity 120). One is called "The Library," and as its name suggests, walls are lined with books plus paintings including one of the original White Rock girl. The second space, called the "Wine Room," recreates the feeling of an Edwardian club. And the third, shown on the following spread, is the "Game Room", its name recalled in mounted stag heads and other animal trophies.

*Copley's Bar, shown on the facing page, was unchanged architecturally. It leads to
a series of three dining rooms, one of which, the "Game Room," is shown above.*

BEL AIR HOTEL

Location: Los Angeles, California
Seating Capacity: 75 (inside); 86 (terrace)
Interior Designer: Louis Cataffo of Intradesign
Photographer: Charles White

The dining room (above) was totally gutted and rebuilt to include French windows that capitalize on views of the surrounding gardens and terrace dining (opposite).

Originally opened in the early 20's as one of the first hotels in Los Angeles, the BEL AIR HOTEL had guests who were primarily East Coast transplants coming for prolonged stays ranging from one to six months. This policy continues even today. Guests feel as if they were in a private retreat, for the BEL AIR is really a glorified bungalow colony with 67 rooms spread throughout eight to ten buildings. Further, the public areas are in three separate structures interconnected by walkways and gardens.

As is all too often the case, the BEL AIR, over the years, had fallen into a sad state of disrepair. It was to be renovated, yet the end result was to appear imperceptible to those who knew the hotel. It was to look as if this were the way it had always been.

The restaurant, which serves three meals daily, retained its original location and configuration, yet was totally gutted and rebuilt. In its "before" state, it had one grotto-like elevation of rocks, all-booth seating and a hodgepodge of small windows. Walls were rebuilt; booths were replaced with tables; French windows were installed to capitalize on views of the gardens and terrace with seating for diners. According to the designer, the gardens are the most spectacular part of the project.

As they are in both public spaces and guest rooms, the furnishings are a mixture of traditional elements and antiques. The latter include a pickled wood mirror frame of 18th-century Italian vintage, an 18th-century console, and a Portuguese rug.

A separate bar, retaining the club like atmosphere of the original, provides an auxilliary area for light dining as well as cocktails. When dining is in order, draped tables are wheeled in to accommodate meals. The seating capacity here is 35-40.

Carpet (custom): Victoria Carpets. *Tables:* Falcon. *Chairs:* Traditional Imports. *Upholstery leather:* Middletown Leather. *Upholstery fabric:* Clarence House. *Drapery fabric and wall covering:* Contex. *Lighting:* CAL Lighting; Minton Spidell. *Outdoor furniture:* Brown Jordan. *Umbrellas:* Wicker Works.

HYATT REGENCY RESTAURANTS

Location: Miami, Florida
Seating Capacity: 108 (Gourmet); 188 (Brasserie)
Interior Designer: Henry End/Michael Arak Assoc.
Photographer: Dan Forer

A tropical theme, native to South Florida, is emphasized by designer Henry End throughout this new Miami hotel, including its two restaurants—the Gourmet Restaurant and the Brasserie. A more casual, relaxed mood is apparent in the Brasserie (shown on this page) with its rattan and bamboo furniture and paneling. The Gourmet Restaurant (opposite page) takes on a more European, formal air with its Chinese Chippendale-style dining chairs, but here, too, the effect is soft and diffused with woven-wood window blinds keeping the atmosphere in tune with the hotel's other public spaces. Lighting is by Howard Brandston-Lighting Design.

Chairs, upholstery fabrics: Shelby Williams. *Brasserie tables:* Falcon. *Tile flooring:* Designers' Tile International. *Carpet:* Gaskell. *Woven wood blinds:* Webb Designs.

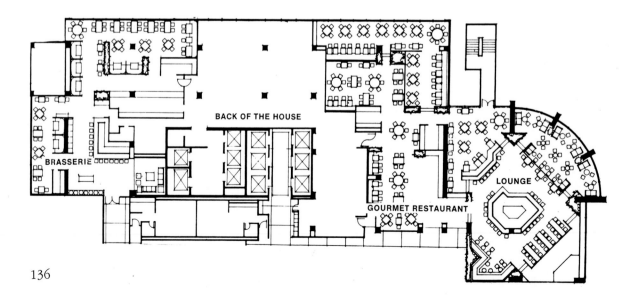

136

ALEXIS HOTEL RESTAURANT

Location: Seattle, Washington
Seating Capacity: 75
Interior Designer: The Bumgardner Architects
Photographer: Dick Busher

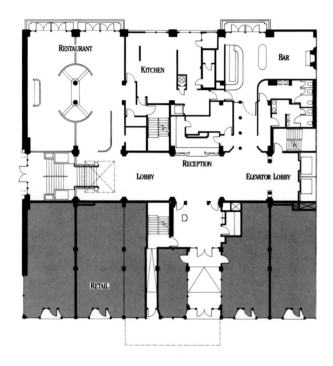

Located in a 1901 building in Seattle's historic waterfront section, this restaurant is part of an overall renovation of the four-story Alexis Hotel. The space is defined by low partition walls with chair rails of plastic laminate. In contrast to the darker, more intimate atmosphere of the adjacent lobby, the restaurant has a light, airy quality. A structural composition formed by the curving light soffits above plaster-veneered columns (formerly timber supports) forms the focal point of the space. Lighting is a combination of recessed incandescents and indirect fluorescents. Madora Lawson, an associate with the architectural firm, headed the interior design group.

Custom chairs: K Downing Imports. *Upholstery fabrics*: Duralee. *Carpet*: Hunter Carpet Mills. *Tables*: Falcon. *Laminate tops*: Nevamar. *Table linens*: J.P. Stevens. *China*: Shenango. *Silver*: Oneida.

Ballrooms

THE HELMSLEY PALACE

Location: New York, New York
Seating Capacity: 350
Interior Designer: Tom Lee Ltd.
Photographer: Jaime Ardiles-Arce

The Versailles Ballroom, although one of the new spaces in the hotel, is nevertheless in the spirit of the historic landmark rooms surrounding it. Oval in shape, it has no divider partitions. Among the decorative highlights are paintings by 19th century French artist Jeanne-Madeleine Le Maire which are placed against moiré-covered walls. Domes in the decorative plaster ceiling muffle sound. The center section of the carpet can be removed for dancing. Because of the huge size of the carpet (it measures 48' by 75' overall), it had to be cut into segments before being flown to New York from its manufacturing site in England and later restitched on location.

Chandeliers: Louis Baldinger & Sons. *Carpet*: Stark. *Architectural woodwork*: John Langenbacher. *Wall covering*: Vicrtex. *Plasterwork*: Saldarini & Pucci. *Paintings*: Florentine Craftsmen.

140

THE PIERRE

Location: New York, New York
Seating Capacity: 750
Interior Designer: Valerian Rybar
Photographer: Jaime Ardiles-Arce

The Grand Ballroom of the Pierre Hotel is designed to suit elegant, formal occasions as well as those of a commercial nature, sit-down dinners as well as a dinner dance. It is also designed to evoke visions of an 18th century Venetian theater, the theme taken from the existing raised esplanade around the perimeter of the room that reminded Rybar of a theater's loge.

In keeping with both the suggested theme and the room's intended functions, Rybar selected traditional furnishings and based his decor scheme on a pale gray/gold color palette. The specially made drapery material is cotton damask with gold overprinting; the wall covering and railing cap are gray velvet; the ceiling has been painted to resemble gold leaf. To overcome a drastic difference in ceiling heights (21 feet for two-thirds of the room; 12 feet for the remaining third), the designer installed a mirrored, draped arch in front of the lower section to conceal it. He then continued this swag treatment around the esplanade, the rationale being that the gold lamé drapery linings could be drawn in front of the "private boxes" for smaller functions in the room.

Recessed lighting is rheostat controlled to service the room's various functions. The chandeliers are custom designs, fabricated in Venice.

Millwork and mirror work: Midhattan Woodworking Corp. *Carpet:* Brintons. *Gray velvet and gold lamé fabrics:* Dazian's. *Vinyl upholstery material:* La France. *Fringe:* Standard Trimming. *Stacking chairs:* Gasser Chair Co. *Cotton fabric:* Pausa.

142

THE WALDORF-ASTORIA

Location: New York, New York
Seating Capacity: 1660
Interior Designer: Kenneth E. Hurd & Associates
Photographer: Nathaniel Lieberman

As part of an on-going renovation program at the Waldorf-Astoria Hotel, the grand ballroom is the latest space to undergo a complete re-do. Although the basic objective was to restore the room to its original classical magnificence (the hotel was built in 1931), the space also had to be updated in several ways with new lighting and sound systems. Restoration work involved removal of the excessive decorative elements which had been added in the 60's and restoring the original Art Deco and Art Nouveau features of the room— the domed ceiling, ornately pierced grillwork, plaster of Paris medallions and reliefs. New elements especially designed for the room—carpeting, lighting and brass railings—are in keeping with the original architecture.

Carpet: BMK of Scotland. *Vinyl wall covering:* Brewster. *Wall sconces:* Custom Lightstyles.

Clubs and Discotheques

Adam Tihany on Clubs

"Normally, eating facilities in clubs have two functions that restaurants do not," says Adam Tihany, designer of such disparate clubs as the discotheque Xenon, the European-styled Club A and the new Playboy Club, all in Manhattan. First, the club restaurant is really a "holding room" for the activities to follow, and in this way differs from the restaurant, where dining represents the evening's focus. Secondly, "people watching" is a top priority activity, and on a par with the dining experience.

Translated into design parlance, these two concepts have several meanings. Ease of circulation is particularly important as people may table-hop or leave in mid-meal to check goings-on in the dance area. Another consideration is the physical positioning of the restaurant within the club. "Normally," Tihany says, "restaurants are put in a location where the people entering the club to dance either must pass through the restaurant or be visible from it." This acts as an incentive for late diners to continue their evening with dancing. Yet another factor has to do with the restaurant's flexibility. In some clubs, the restaurant must go through changes as the evening progresses and the clientele's focus shifts. First, the restaurant functions as a standard dining room until about 10:30 or 11:00 and should be separated from the club either with physical partitions or suggestive elements like lighting. Later, the restaurant may be absorbed into the club proper, allowing diners to dance and still keep their tables for drinks.

There are several options for dining facilities in clubs. A private club, such as Club A (see pages 148-151), may have a restaurant for members only, or it may have one that is open to the public and operates as a freestanding facility. Club A has both. The brasserie-styled facility for members only is a glass-enclosed extension of the dance area. Tucano, the fine dining facility, is physically separate from the club and has its own private entry. But, the restaurant also offers direct access to the club without having to exit the premises. Financially, says Tihany, it is risky business to have a members-only restaurant, particularly in large cities where outside competition is strong. But on the other hand, a restaurant adds prestige value to both the club and its patrons, particularly when entertaining for business purposes.

Clubs and their dining facilities aim for as many off-hour activities as possible to increase profits. Some have private dining facilities conceived to cater to an active lunchtime clientele. Other alternatives are to have these restaurants available for private functions like catered luncheons, private parties or fashion shows, a natural because of the availability of sophisticated lighting and sound systems. This multi-use potential influences certain design

elements. Lighting is most important. It must be flexible enough to create a sophisticated daytime restaurant ambience as well as evening excitement. "There's nothing worse than night club lighting during the day," says Tihany. Certain elements, most commonly table tops, are changed according to the event taking place. Table tops are larger during the day, giving diners increased space, and smaller at night so that more people can be packed into the room. Finally, there is that intangible element called mood. "You have to be able to play with the space's mood," Tihany comments.

As with any business, identification of the client is crucial to its success. Nowhere may this be truer than with clubs. But planning a club's concept entails more than identifying prospective patrons. It requires experience and a totally accurate sense of the times. For example, six or seven years ago, the large discotheques were created for a young, trendy crowd. There were no dining facilities; even drinking was minimal. Therefore, admission fees represented the source of profits and had to be calculated accordingly. Recently the mood has changed. Supper clubs, where profits come from dining and particularly drinking, are in. "The reason these clubs exist is that people got tired of the abuses of places like Studio 54 and Xenon," he says. "Now people are looking for comfort, luxury and romance." These clubs have an aura of exclusivity, partially maintained by steep prices: $10-$30 for entrance fees; $5-$10 per drink; approximately $1000 for membership fees.

But the money must be made quickly as longevity is limited, and unless the facility is private, it is difficult to establish a loyal clientele. The average life-cycle for a discotheque without dining is two or three years; for a facility with dining, the time frame increases to an average of five years.

Commenting briefly on differences between European and American establishments, Tihany remarks that club-going in Europe is a social activity geared more toward couples. In this country, clubs draw a big singles crowd. Consequently, American clubs are designed for faster and easier eye contact. They are generally on one level with few hide-away niches for intimate conversation. American dance floors tend to occupy a good percentage of the overall area as dancing is the focal activity. In contrast, dancing in Europe is more of a supplementary activity to conversation and drinks among friends. European club owners may stand to make more money as drinks offer a sizeable profit margin.

Design, concept, quality of food aside, there is one additional factor, a sine qua non, for a club's success. This, Tihany concludes, is the media.

ADAM TIHANY, who received architectural training in Milan has a long list of both residential and commercial interiors to his credit as well as product designs. Current or just-completed projects include: DDL Foodshow, Los Angeles; the Drake Hotel, New York; the Doubletree Inn, Phoenix.

CLUB A

Location: New York, New York
Seating Capacity: 120(Tucano); 30(private dining); 60(bistro)
Interior Designer: Adam Tihany and Robert Couturier
Photographer: Mark Ross

In Manhattan's crush of discotheques and clubs, both private and public, Club A stands alone. It is an amalgam of a classy, public restaurant plus a private night club with steep membership fees. In design, it is a custom project with a good percentage of the elements fabricated in Italy to cirumvent tight scheduling—six months of planning and five months of construction.

This is a project where the client, based on his extensive experience, had a great deal of input. Club A is one of the recent night

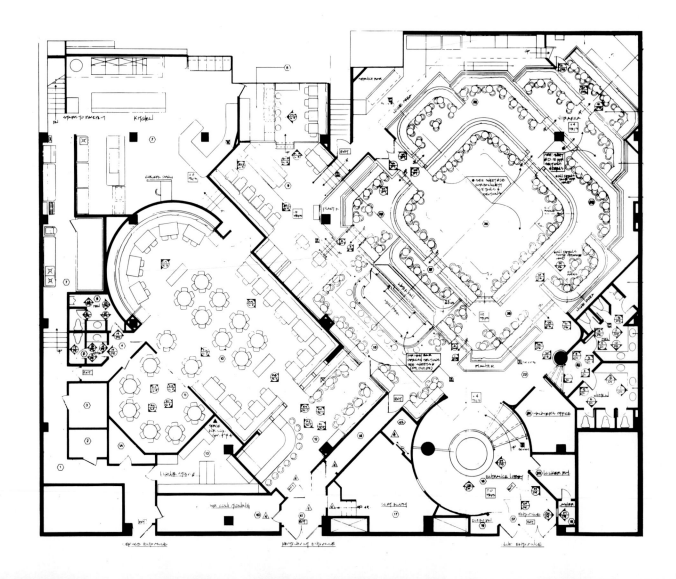

ground. In addition, an internal pass-through between restaurant and club was required so that diners could proceed to dancing without exiting the premises. Circulation, then, was crucial not only for front-of-the-house premises, but also behind the scenes. Here, two separate kitchens were called for to service each of the restaurant facilities.

Overall, the space has a diagonal orientation, the solution providing for the largest span between two structural columns for the dance floor (18 feet square). On the left is the formal restaurant Tucano which also features a private dining room for parties of up to 30. It also has its own small bar/lounge, separated from the adjacent night club by a one-way mirror that enables diners to see into the club without being seen in return. Tucano's atmosphere might be described as tropical chic: strong colors for the carpeting and striped velvet upholstery fabric; exotic pearwood paneling; a mirrored ceiling; murals of brilliantly colored tropical birds; and whimsical lighting sconces of oversized glass fruits, hand-blown in Venice.

Between the restaurant and night club are the latter's bar and the bistro. An unusual feature of the club is its ceiling treatment, a multi-leveled plane of interlocking forms designed to conceal lighting and sound equipment. As is fitting, the bar is the focal point. It is a spectacular element of curved, etched glass, topped with glass trees and backed by an 18-foot-high waterfall. The bistro, called Bar de Theatre, is glass enclosed and tucked away in a raised corner. Wood flooring, a stamped metal ceiling, country French antiques and candle lighting provide a break from the otherwise pervasive hard-edged chic, and establish the requisite theme which is supported by the menu.

spots opened by Brazilian pro Ricardo Amaral, owner of analogous operations in Argentina and Paris as well as in his native country. Amaral came to Tihany with a precise concept of what he wanted: a club following the European tradition of sit-down table service for drinks around a center-stage dance floor; a fine restaurant for before-dance dining; a casual bistro-style facility with light fare to appease members' late evening hunger pangs. What he did not have was a site.

Together, designer and client settled on a 15,000-square-foot empty loft structure on the Upper East Side. Establishing a floor plan that would meet all the requirements of these interrelated sectors presented the most challenge. Provisions were to be made for separate entries to both restaurant and club. Entry to the latter is marked by a suitably dramatic 25-foot diameter well surrounded by lush foliage that first establishes the appropriate tropical theme reflecting the client's back-

General contractor: Wildman & Bernhardt. *Custom cabinetry*: Capital Cabinet. *Lighting consultant*: Litelab. *Sound consultant*: Richard Long Assoc. *Custom seating*: Weissman Heller. *Mirrored ceiling*: Lancer Metal & Glass Works. *Carpet*: Stark. *Custom shades and canopy*: Tony Rizzolo. *Fabric* (shade and canopy): Westgate.

The public restaurant Tucano is linked to the private dancing area of Club A by a sliding door in the restaurant's cocktail lounge (below). The tropical motif of the restaurant is established by murals and blown glass fruit sconces custom made in Venice. The club proper, (previous spread) features table service for drinks as do European clubs.

TOUCH

Location: Beverly Hills, California
Seating Capacity: 130
Interior Designer: Stanley Felderman
Photographer: Toshi Yoshimi

Touch, a private club with dining and dancing facilities, derives its name from the character of the place which was conceived primarily for people who prefer "touch" to disco dancing. It is a concept which suggests romance, luxury and elegance, a concept interpreted by the designer in elements of Art Nouveau inspiration.

The space involved 8,000 square feet (1,500 of them added) to what had been a Chinese restaurant. The former rectangular plan of the restaurant was retained for major function areas. Mirrors, sand-blasted glass partitions and romantic murals by artist Dennis Abbé provide the main decorative elements in the dining room. Seating is divided into two areas—a smaller section adjacent to the bar, and a large, main dining space. Mahogany columns with brass banding provide a recurring architectural theme, some of them used for support, others merely to define space. Soft task and ambient lighting helps create a feeling of intimacy.

In the dance area, flooring is marble under a fan-shaped skylight which rises to 26′ in height.

Carpet: Edward Fields. *Dining seating:* Northwestern Showcase. *Lounge seating:* Kasparians. *Bar stools:* Shelby Williams. *Hanging light fixtures:* Gruen Lighting. *Marble floor:* North Hollywood Marble Co.

At right: entrance to the club is through a brass-decorated door which pivots so that it seems to "float" inward. On the opposite page: a view through the door to the bar. Overleaf: a view of the main dining space as seen through a sand-blasted glass partition.

152

Shown on the facing page is a view of the marble-floor dance space under a 26' high skylight. Seen in the view of the main dining room below is the hand-painted mural by Dennis Abbé which spans one wall.

DOUBLES

Location: New York, New York
Seating Capacity: 70-85 (luncheon/game room); 120-150 (disco/dining)
Interior Designer: Valerian Rybar
Photographer: Jaime Ardiles-Arce

DOUBLES, located in the sub-street level of the Sherry Netherland Hotel on Fifth Avenue, is a venerable establishment aimed at well-to-do patrons of a particular status. It is decidedly not for the punk or hard rock disco crowd, nor is it for New York's relentlessly trendy set. Instead, it is a private club designed with a gaming room and luncheon facility to function by day, and a room for a supper club/discotheque by night. In addition to these two large rooms, there are separate entry and lounge spaces. As expected, each room is designed to evoke a distinctly different atmosphere. Yet elements such as color and an abundance of mirror and shiny metal for detailing unify the rooms.

The gaming room is on two levels and has both table and alcove/booth seating. Luncheon meals are served buffet style at the designer's suggestion. "This is a club where most of the people know one another, and buffet service encourages interaction among them," Rybar says. Based on its function, the room has a sober yet elegant tone achieved through a dark brown and red lacquer palette with brass for detailing. A sliding panel door cut into the common wall allows the room to be conjoined with the adjacent discotheque to provide patrons with a quiet zone as an alternative to the disco/dining scene.

A counterpoint, this second facility is brilliant red and hard-edged glitter. Columns, the ceiling perimeter and the floating ceiling over the dance floor are mirrored; additional architectural detailing is chrome finished. Again, both chair and banquette seating is used, the latter adhering to residential proportions. Lighting comes from recessed spots and table candles; speakers are concealed in the floating ceiling.

General contractor: Ambassador Construction. *Carpet:* Couristan. *Lighting:* Lighting Services; Lighting Associates; Greene Bros.; Koch & Lowy. *Tables, cocktail tables, banquettes, bar (custom):* Chairmasters. *Settees:* Ben Feibusch. *Vinyl wall and ceiling covering:* Naugahyde by Uniroyal. *Lounge chairs:* Driver Desk Company. *Dining chairs:* Shelby Williams. *Fabrics:* Cohama Specifier; Mira X; Stroheim & Romann.

The gaming room and luncheon facility is used during the day as is the cocktail lounge shown on the preceding page. Meals are served buffet style to encourage interaction among club members. A sliding panel door allows this room to be conjoined with the adjacent room, which functions as a discotheque and supper club.

160

BOCCACCIO

Location: Houston, Texas
Seating Capacity: 70 (dining room)
Interior Designer: Creative Environs
Photographer: Hickey-Robertson

The client—restaurateur Mike Steinmann—was specific in his requirements: create a private club with disco and dining in 5,260 square feet of space formerly occupied by a fast-food restaurant. The envisioned clientele: the international jet set.

The first step was to gut and restructure the interior; only the kitchen and one bar were retained. The client's principal concept—that there be visual access to the dance floor from any point in the club—was the starting point for subsequent design decisions. The restaurant and dance/lounge sectors, therefore, are not physically separated, but flow together with divisions suggested through changes in levels, furnishings, color and lighting. Although there are no partitions per se, there are semi-private niches, or "breakaway" spaces so that patrons can gather to converse in small groups but still see the action.

The design theme is a subtle recalling of Art Deco in the etched glass and furniture forms as well as in the sculptural shape of the space itself with its skillfull blending of built-in furnishings and architecture.

Lighting, one of the most important elements in a project of this kind, also helps to separate the entertainment and dining areas—the discotheque being dimly lit with capabilities of many theatrical variations; recessed museum spotlights used in the lounge; and recessed bulbs placed over individual tables in the dining area.

Principals responsible for the project were Mary MacDonald, vice president/design and Jerry Szwed, vice president/architecture. The general contractor was Tony Salvaggio.

Dining, cocktail tables, bar stools: Shelby Williams. *Upholstery fabrics:* Frankel Fabrics; Boris Kroll. *Carpet:* Harbinger. *Discotheque lighting:* Tivoli. *Wall sconces:* Metropolitan Lighting. *Etched glass:* Joan of Art. *China:* Fitz & Floyd.

162

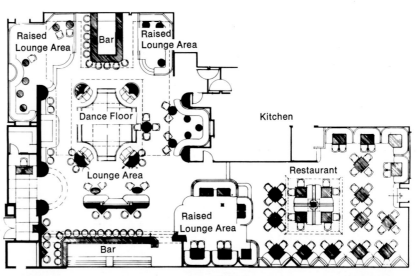

Raised Lounge Area

Bar

Raised Lounge Area

Dance Floor

Kitchen

Lounge Area

Restaurant

Raised Lounge Area

Bar

Serpentine-shaped banquettes separate the raised lounge area from the restaurant which also has a lighter color palette and higher level of lighting than the discotheque.

GIRARD'S

Location: Baltimore, Maryland
Interior Designer: Bromley/Jacobsen
Photographer: Jaime Ardiles-Arce

On the facing page is a view from the lounge looking into the cafe section which is far enough from the dance floor (shown on the following two pages) to make conversation possible.

The requirements set forth by the clients were to create a discotheque that had all the vitality of New York's Studio 54 but was more than just a place to dance. They wanted to evoke the atmosphere of a private club by offering food service in a small cafe sector and to provide lounge seating.

Physically, the space encompasses a series of three conjoined buildings, originally an automobile showroom. This presented the most immediate design problem—the replacement of the exterior glass walls. The designer chose porcelain metal panels of Mirawall which repeat the same deep green color used for the interior background.

Inside, the rectangularity of the space was alleviated by the angular placement of banquette seating and the bar, and by a slight change in levels. The main lounge and cafe, just beyond the entrance, are on one level. Additional lounge seating is three steps down; beyond that is the dance floor, down still another step. This spatial delineation places the cafe far enough from the dance floor so that conversation is not drowned out by disco music.

The architectural lighting, designed by Brian Thompson, is based on low voltage incandescent lamps, with one transformer for every 20 lights. Thompson uses color in his lighting scheme, mixing it to produce white light, or using single hues to wash certain areas with a distinct glow—lavender in the lounge and red in the cafe and kitchen. The kinetic discotheque lighting was designed by Paul Marantz of Jules Fisher & Paul Marantz. The sound system is by Paul Friedman of G.L.I. Associates.

Banquette seating: Ibello-Rifici. *Upholstery and wall panel canvas:* John Boyle. *Dining chairs:* Abitare. *Lacquered cocktail tables:* Jacob Froelich Cabinet Works. *Carpet:* Stratton. *Dance floor:* Artisan Flooring. *Lighting fixtures:* Lighting, Inc.

166

Two views, taken from the entrance, showing the
primary lounge area and a view towards the
dance floor. The bar has a bullnose edge of stained
beech and a carpeted fascia.

CLYDE'S AT TYSONS CORNER

With a seating capacity of 75, this bar and adjacent lounge area are a superb recreation of an elaborate turn-of-the-century design. The glow of rich red mahogany is highlighted by panels of back-lit Plexiglas suggesting the look of tortoise shell. Flooring is Mexican clay tile. Adding to the authenticity are an embossed tin ceiling, lighting fixtures with art glass shades and intricate wood carvings. John Richards Andrews was the designer.

Tin ceiling: C. A. Ohman & Co. *Bar, bar stools:* Artcraft Woodworking. *Glass light shades:* George Thiewes. *Photographer:* Mark Ross

LE RENDEZ-VOUS

Angled bars offer a good seating arrangement without a railroad effect as illustrated in this Chicago restaurant bar designed by Spiros Zakas. The bar is padded and covered with vinyl suede.

Bar stools: ICF. *Fabrics:* Stroheim & Romann. *Carpet:* Jack KorNick & Associates. *Photographer:* Idaka.

WALDORF-ASTORIA COCKTAIL LOUNGE

Location: New York, New York
Seating Capacity: 80
Interior Designer: Kenneth E. Hurd & Associates
Photographer: Jaime Ardiles-Arce

Finding ways to make better use of existing space to provide increased revenue is a problem common to all hotels. The venerable Waldorf-Astoria is no exception, and the hotel's most recent step in that direction was the decision to take the terrace area of the Park Avenue lobby, which was being used to store banquet equipment, and convert it into a cocktail lounge.

In working on the project, designer Kenneth E. Hurd convinced management that the adjoining lobby should be considered as an integral part of the overall plan, and a total renovation program was undertaken. The original Art Deco decoration of the space, most of which had been well preserved but merely covered up, was revealed and new elements designed that were compatible with it. As a focal point on the terrace, shown on the facing page, a pavilion structure was designed and a grand piano added to attract people as they pass through the lobby on their way to Park Avenue. In the four corners of the pavilion are etched glass panels with Art Deco figures.

Millwork: Architectural Interiors. *Carpet:* Bloomsburg. *Lounge chairs:* David-Edward. *Etched glass panels:* Shefts Bros.

176

Historic
Restorations

SHERMAN'S TAVERNE BY THE GREEN

Location: New Haven, Connecticut
Seating Capacity: 100 (dining room)
Interior Designer: Marcel Bretos
Photographer: Mark Ross

Above the fireplace in the main dining room (opposite) is a plaque testifying to the visit by George Washington in 1789.

The building which houses Sherman's Taverne by the Green has had a long and varied history beginning as the home of Roger Sherman, New Haven's first mayor. At the turn of the century, it was converted for use as a men's club, and a reception hall was added at that time which is now the main dining room. Before its current restoration, it was used as a cabaret, and some of the additions made then, such as the brick bar, were retained. Otherwise, according to the designer, it was a matter of "reclamation, recoloring and organization clarification of existing space."

The Taverne is divided into three main areas: the dining room to the front, the kitchen in the rear, and the bar in between. A large brass chandelier lights the bar; wall sconces and hanging lanterns provide supplemental lighting in the surrounding area. Crystal chandeliers are used in the dining room. Except in the kitchen, there are no fluorescents.

Heavily varnished oak paneling in the dining room was stripped and refinished and brightened with panels of mirror. The marble columns, pilasters and fireplace surround were restored. The existing stained-glass transoms over the windows, doors and fireplace were decorative assets and needed only to be cleaned and backlit.

Carpet: Brintons. *Brass chandeliers:* Lester Berry. *Sconces:* Virginia Metalcrafters; Norman Perry. *Tables and dining chairs:* Broyhill. *Bar stools:* Lenore Chair. *Glassware:* Baccarat. *Flatware:* International Silver. *Linen:* Kemp & Beattle.

179

The bar area (this page) and the dining room (facing page) are next to one another and are of approximately equal size. The furnishings in each were selected to conform to the general character of the spaces. A large brass chandelier hangs over the brick bar. The paneling and stained glass in the dining room were existing and restored to their original condition.

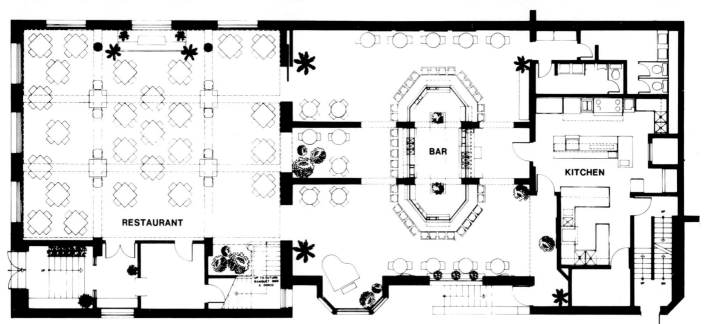

RESTAURANT

BAR

KITCHEN

UP TO FUTURE
BANQUET RMS
& DISCO

181

GADSBY'S TAVERN

Location: Alexandria, Virginia
Seating Capacity: 30 (Tap Room)
Interior Designer: Edward C. Plyler, ASID
Photographer: Jaime Ardiles-Arce

The history of this restored landmark goes back to 1752 when a city tavern was erected in Alexandria, Virginia. George Washington occupied it as his headquarters on three occasions; Lafayette was given a banquet there; and many other notable gentlemen were entertained there. The tavern takes its name from John Gadsby, an Englishman who owned a coach line and acquired the property in 1793.

Over the years, the tavern underwent several phases of deterioration and renovation, and much of its original interior architecture, including the ballroom, was purchased by the Metropolitan Museum. In 1930, it was acquired by the American Legion which subsequently presented the building to the city of Alexandria with the understanding that the city would restore it. A small section of the building is still used by the Legion.

Its restoration involved a number of forces starting with a Friends of Gadsby's Committee. Edward C. Plyler, ASID, donated his services to help restore the interiors, and he formed a small committee from the Potomac Chapter of the American Society of Interior Designers to work with him.

The Tap Room (on the facing page), is one of three dining areas in the tavern. The mantel is original to the house and was brought back from the Metropolitan Museum which had acquired it earlier. All furniture was made by Virginia craftsmen.

GENERAL ACCIDENT INSURANCE COMPANY

Location: Philadelphia, Pennsylvania
Seating Capacity: 300
Interior Designer: Kenneth Parker Associates
Photographer: Tom Crane

The bright airy garden theme of the General Accident Insurance Company's employee cafeteria was planned as a pleasant counterpoint to the workday environment of a landscaped system. Although the 7,500-square foot space of rectangular configuration seats 300, it is planned like a restaurant with more intimate seating areas·suggested by the waist-high dividers and painted columns that break up the area. Decorative elements establishing the motif include air-brushed flower murals by Peter Freudenberg, gazebos and garden umbrellas. The cafeteria is open as early as 6:00 AM for breakfast service and continues operation for most of the day.

Ceramic tile: Buchtal through Diener Buck Co. *Chairs:* Buckstaff. *Tables:* Johnson Industries. *Upholstery vinyl:* Naugahyde by Uniroyal. *Light tubes:* Lightolier.

186

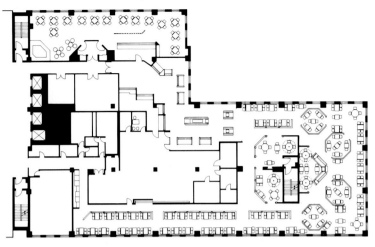

XEROX
CORPORATION

Location: Stamford, Connecticut
Seating Capacity: 264
Interior Designer: ISD Incorporated
Photographer: Jaime Ardiles-Arce

The company cafeteria in the new headquarters building of Xerox is one of the focal points of the 250,000 square foot facility. Located in a four-story skylit atrium, it has the atmosphere of a festive marketplace achieved through the use of bright colors and a multi-plane fiberwork sculpture by Gerhardt Knodel comprised of silver, gold and clear Mylar with wool fibers, suspended from the atrium by means of a cord system. Seating, including the partitions, is entirely movable and appears to be randomly placed rather than adhering to a rigid grid system.

Carpet: Bigelow. *Tables:* Kinetics. *Dining chairs:* Stendig. *Custom banquettes:* William Somerville/Chairmasters. *Hanging lamps:* Atelier International. *Carpet on walls:* Patrick Mills.

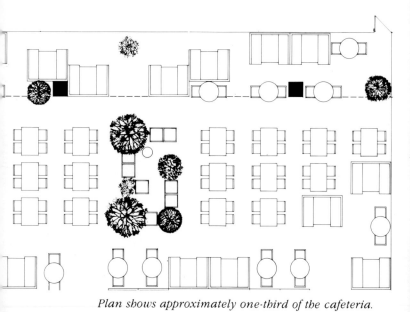

Plan shows approximately one-third of the cafeteria.

INTERNATIONAL PAPER COMPANY

Location: New York, New York
Seating Capacity: 300 (large dining room); 100 (small dining room)
Interior Designer: The Space Design Group
Photographer: Mark Ross

Two dining facilities are open to all International Paper employees—the larger one cafeteria style (opposite page), the smaller one with waitress service (below). Both are situated off the employee lounge and are served from a large kitchen and smaller pantry. Located on the 35th floor, they offer a panoramic view of midtown Manhattan and are left open and unobstructed. To make the space more intimate and human in scale, however, ceiling heights were varied and reflective metal ceilings added. In the larger dining space, seating is varied by combining booths, tables for two and four, as well as larger tables for twelve. Both dining areas are carpeted.

Carpet: Mort West Mills. *Tables:* L & B Products. *Metal ceilings:* Alcan Building Products. *Chairs (small dining room):* Knoll; *(large dining room):* ICF. *Cabinetry:* Jaff Bros.

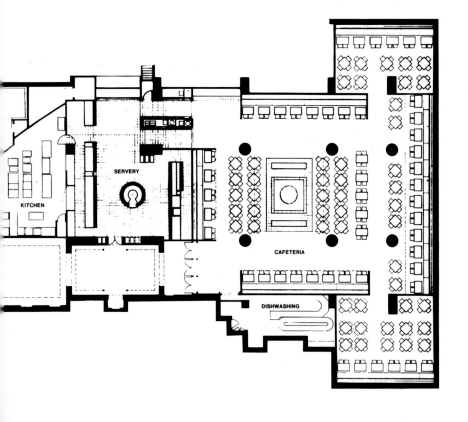

PHILIP MORRIS WORLD HEADQUARTERS

Location: New York, New York
Seating Capacity: 440
Interior Designer: Ulrich Franzen, FAIA
Photographer: Norman McGrath

To create the illusion of being outdoors in this below-ground cafeteria, the designers ringed the walls with a series of cityscape murals by Richard Haas. An illuminated fountain in the center of the space continues the outdoor image. Francoise Bollack was design coordinator.

Tables: ICF. *Chairs:* Stendig. *Fabric covers:* Knoll Textiles. *Carpet:* Bloomsburg Industries. *Lighting:* Lightolier. *Fountain:* Eastern Architectural Systems.

The Grand Cafe: Why It Failed

All the elements were right. Decor. Food. Location. Service. The Art Deco-styled interiors, based on extensive background research of the period, took on the quality of a restoration rather than a stage-set. For Joseph Villano of Aquarius Designs Ltd. attended to the most minute detail, from the ombréd walls to the three-color detailing on moldings, blue mirror accents and etched glass panels. In fact, when *New York Times* critic John Canaday reviewed the restaurant just two weeks after its opening, he began his piece giving kudos to the decor. The rave review continued to the food, concluding with a four-star rating. In the history of the Times' restaurant reviews, it was a rare phenomenon to garner so much favorable publicity so soon.

Indeed, there were special touches—to both menu and operating style. There was, for example, a full roster of both American and French styled cuisine with one side devoted to each. Patrons, offered a special wine-tasting service, were presented with liqueur-sized glasses and a carrier of six wines from which to sample before ordering. Attention was paid to such serving details as demitasse spoons and plates of fruit and cheese at the end of a meal. Overall, a sense of great style prevailed.

Of the other elements influencing success—location and service, both seemed proper. THE GRAND CAFE was located in the core of Manhattan's Upper East Side from where it intended to draw a good percentage of the wealthy clientele that it sought. Even so, location is rarely a factor in Manhattan. New Yorkers will go anywhere, from Tribecca to the Upper West Side, to be part of a new "in" restaurant crowd. Of late, the more out of the way a restaurant is, the more people flock to it as if members of an elite club of cognoscenti. Finally, the service, although not without flaws, was judged to be competent. Says Villano, "It was a magical place. It would have been something that people wanted to see." Even if it had eventually lost its appeal to the natives and attracted primarily a tourist trade, that is still business that cannot be discounted. In its first few months when at least a week's advance booking was required, THE GRAND CAFE served almost 500 meals daily—a lunch and two dinner seatings to a capacity of 140.

PHOTOGRAPHER: LOUIS REENS

THE GRAND CAFE lasted less than a year. Sadly, its demise began almost simultaneously with its spectacular opening success. What went wrong? Was it a victim of its own popularity? Was it the casualty of a fickle public? Doubtfully so in either case. Villano, in a most candid conversation, analyzes the mistakes and shortcomings from the vantage point of hindsight and gained experience.

To understand the failings, one need first know the background and concept. For most first-time owners, a restaurant represents the opportunity to fulfill certain dreams. This couple was no exception. But they were inexperienced and knew it. Recognizing their naivete, they brought in a successful restaurateur as a partner. He was the owner and creator of the singles bar phenomena Friday's, and later Tuesday's and Thursday's, as well as owner of the more recent and popular steakhouse Smith & Wollensky's. Although failure in any business comes from an interplay of factors, the failure in this case began here. From the start, each had a different idea of what THE GRAND CAFE should be. For Ray and Madelaine Senter, it was to be the epitome of high-styled dining. Perhaps they harbored visions of creating another New York institution along the lines of Lutece. Their partner, on the other hand, favored a cafe in the more informal sense of the word with a brasserie styled menu and decor scheme. Starting with initial disapproval of the salmon based color palette that was crucial to the setting and overall concept, he never wholeheartedly came to terms with the Senters' plan. Villano, who had never before designed a restaurant, was in no position to intermediate.

In two words, operations and attitude, held the keys to failure. The partner, drawing on his experience with successful restaurants although of a decidedly different caliber, held the opinion that people will eat anything if the environment is attractive. Even if they are paying top dollar for it. So, in order to reduce a steep overhead, he began to cut back on the quality of the food. Cutbacks were subtle, but they didn't escape the attention of the public that expected the first-rate food on which THE GRAND CAFE based its image. There were also management related difficulties. At first, the Senters remained on-site prior to, during and after the restaurant's operating hours. Understandedly, this pace became too grueling to live with. And the partner believed that operations would not be too adversely affected without one of the owners present at all times. He was proved wrong. Without a dedicated staff, service is bound to deteriorate, and in this case it did. Perhaps if the owners had been able to instill a sense of the staff's importance in the restaurant's success, things might have been otherwise. But the lapses, in combination with the suffering quality of food, were enough to tarnish severely the image. This laissez-faire attitude became even more apparent later. As the coup de grace, the chef was not replaced when he left. Instead, what was once a four-star restaurant operated under the direction of only a sous-chef. During this period the power of the New York restaurant critic again came into play. Mimi Sheraton's review, pointing out the succession of shortcomings, was confirmation of the internal politics that were held responsible.

Could THE GRAND CAFE have been saved? Maybe, if treated in time by an outside party. Could it have been resurrected? Doubtfully so given its extreme high and subsequent low. The lessons are obvious. But perhaps what is less obvious are the interpersonal relationships on which a successful operation rides. Their consideration in hindsight often arrives too late.

Mary MacDonald on Budgeting

In the hospitality design field, the objective of a good design team is to create a profitable property for the client. To do so requires not only interior design skills but also marketing knowledge in that field.

In establishing a budget, it is not merely a question of how much money should be dedicated to design but what is the proper allocation of that money. For example, it may satisfy the ego of a designer to spend a large sum of money for a brilliantly designed piece of custom furniture, but if it is too sophisticated for the type of restaurant being planned, it is a waste of money. It is better to concentrate on putting the money where it shows as a feature and saving money on a table top which will always be covered with linen. The goal of the designer should always be: spend the budget profitably per seat according to the established design concept.

Budgeting in restaurant design is accomplished in many phases. With the initial design proposal, it can be formulated on a dollar per square foot or a per seat basis. If the designer is presented with an architectural plan and no seating layout, he will probably figure the budget on a square foot basis. On the other hand, if the client states in the beginning that he wants a certain type of restaurant that will seat "x" number of people, the budget figure will be based on a per seat basis. In the latter case, the designer should be able from experience to determine what the cost will be by going through his files and getting the figures of restaurants he has designed in a similar style.

During preliminary design phases, floor plans are developed and an inventory-type budget is prepared. This will make note of any demolition, construction, millwork, finishes, wall coverings, carpeting and furniture selections.

In doing this, it is essential always to add a contingency figure to allow for the unexpected ("It will always be needed."). Creative Environs adds 10% on new construction and up to 20% on a renovation project. The greater percentage is used on a renovation or remodeling job, since many problems often arise which cannot be anticipated: "When you start removing previous renovations—tearing down walls in front of other walls—you never know what lies beyond." The budget should also always include any purchasing fees, sales tax, shipping and delivery.

Where do the numbers come from? There are no industry standards. In fact, the only standards are the variables. Vast differences apply to new construction versus renovation. A hotel restaurant is budgeted differently than a free-standing one.

It is ordinarily easier to pinpoint a budget for new construction. A check list should be provided by the designer showing those elements in the budget which are to be provided by the general contractor and those to be provided by the designer. In general, anything which will be permanently affixed to the building will be in the general contractor's budget. On new construction, the general contractor will install flooring, mirrored walls and allow for extra weight in the ceiling if chandeliers are to be hung. Some areas may overlap such as decorative hardware or wall coverings which are usually selected and purchased by the designer but installed by the general contractor. Other elements may be specified by the designer but included in the general contractor's budget: changes in floor levels or partitioning are two examples.

It is also the designer's responsibility to help guide the client into creating the kind of restaurant that is best suited for the expected patronage. Many food and beverage directors in hotels want to make their restaurant as deluxe and sophisticated as possible. But that type of restaurant may be wrong. In a commercial hotel, for example, a casual steak and seafood restaurant may be more appropriate—and profitable—than a very elegant restaurant with an authentic French menu. Every interior designer wants to please his client, for he is the one paying the bills. But he also should try to keep him from making mistakes and to help him create a property that will be profitable.

MARY MACDONALD was formerly vice president and senior designer at Creative Environs, a design firm located in Coral Gables, Florida. Her background includes not only a degree in interior design but also a B.S. in hospitality management.

199

CASE STUDY

Project: Aux Chantilly Cabaret
Location: New Orleans, Louisiana

CASE STUDY

Project: Lalique
Location: Bal Harbour, Florida

The three-story restaurant, built within a landmark warehouse structure, is planned with a French 1930's-styled cabaret on the first floor and dining rooms on the second and third stories. These are all intimate rooms which range from private residential-like dining rooms with fireplaces to a Garden Room open to the elements. The budget of $461,018 was for furniture, fixtures and equipment only. Since the interiors were essentially a new construction, the building, walls, stairway, skylight, fireplaces and hard-surface flooring were part of the general contractor's budget but designed by Creative Environs. Tabletop accessories and kitchens were in the kitchen budget.

Square footage: 7,280
Square footage cost: $63.00
Seats: 250
Cost per seat: $1,850.00

Located in the Bal Harbour Americana, this restaurant was part of an $18 million renovation program undertaken by Sheraton. A budget of $385,000 was allocated to convert the former Gaucho Steak House into a gourmet "signature" restaurant for the hotel. The budget included demolition, construction, lighting, furniture, etched glass and accessories. It did not include the kitchen, service stations or CLUGS (China, linen, uniforms, glassware and silver). Outstanding features are upholstered walls, an abundant use of etched glass, custom sconces and lighting. (For other design details and interior views, see pages 66-69).

Square footage: 1,988
Square footage cost: $201
Seats: 122
Cost per seat: $3,280

CASE STUDY

Project: Boccaccio
Location: Houston, Texas

HICKEY-ROBERTSON

CASE STUDY

Project: Cartouche
Location: Chicago, Illinois

HEDRICH-BLESSING, LTD

The assignment was to covert a former "Pronto" restaurant into a posh private club with disco and dining for $350,000 complete. This figure was to include all demolition, construction, millwork and furnishings. It did not include the kitchen, bar equipment, CLUGS (china, linen, uniforms, glassware and silver) or the sound system. Other areas designed but not in the budget: exterior facade, exterior lighting, graphics and tabletop design. (For other design details and interior views, see pages 162-165).

Square footage: 5,264
Square footage cost: $66.48
Seats: 193
Cost per seat: $1,813

This was a major renovation project in the former Chicago Sheraton Hotel which had been purchased by the Radisson Hotel Corporation. The overall budget was set at $1 million. The ground floor was completely gutted to accommodate a street level entrance and one all-purpose restaurant created to serve convention patronage. Level changes in the existing foundation varied as much as 16″ which suggested the design of one large restaurant, divided into several areas, related in theme but changed in mood and atmosphere.

Square footage: 4,250
Square footage cost: $235
Seats: 225
Cost per seat: $4,000

Milton Glaser on Graphics

"Graphics are like everything else. They are one of the mechanisms of design used to create the spirit of a place. The objectives of graphics and interior design are the same; the two are not fundamentally different activities." This from preeminent graphic designer Milton Glaser whose list of credits in severely edited form includes: Windows on the World, the King Cole Room at New York's St. Regis hotel, a complex of restaurants at Kansas City's Crown Center, and the co-founding with Clay Felker of *New York* magazine.

When Glaser talks about graphics and menu design, he does so in the context of the entire restaurant and the dining experience it offers. A successful graphics program is not just one that looks attractive. It is one that has bearing on virtually every aspect of a restaurant—from the subjective image-forming aspect to the tangible ordering of a meal. Graphics are also part of the package that reinforces the color scheme, complements the table top appointments, and contributes to the marketing plan.

First, graphics must begin with a clear idea of what they are to achieve. Just as the interior design must. "That primary goal is to attract people, make them comfortable, and let them feel rewarded by the dining experience," he says. "And the obvious elements here are food and service. They must be appropriate for the audience and imply a sense of value. All the other elements of interior design and graphics advance to emphasize the concept. Graphics help to create the personality of the place." Analysis of some of his own projects illustrated here helps to make the point.

Sneakers, part of a health club in a Florida condominium complex, was created to be a lively unintimidating luncheon club for members before or after they exercise. The menu cover, bright with primary colors and a bold logotype, reinforces the informality. A menu can suggest a sense of special care and quality devoted to the food, even in a fast-food operation. Such is the case for the Delicatessan in the Crown Center Complex, Kansas City. The pamphlet-styled piece has an index-tabbed page for each food category (sandwiches, hot platters, salads, beverages, desserts), clear bold typography and an eye-catching blue cover. Clearly the owners cared enough to have a professional design the piece. This is the message perceived by patrons. And clearly the owners care enough to devote above-average attention to the quality of the food. This is the subliminal message suggested by the menu. Without being condescending, a menu can help educate a clientele that may be unfamiliar with the featured style of cuisine. At Crawdaddy's in New York's Biltmore Hotel, Creole cooking is the specialty. Glaser's menu, in addition to listing dishes, incorporates a glossary of relevant terms.

A menu need not be lavish or expensive to make a point. In fact, Glaser created a simple throw-away item as a psychological aid to the marketing plan for The Market restaurant at the World Trade Center. Here, the concept had the restaurant created as a place where patrons were to find the best individual type of food—selected daily according to what the market had to bear and purchased from that purveyor offering the finest quality. The menu helps to make the point. Designed as a simple typewritten sheet of paper to be changed daily, it has eight panel columns where the supplier of each food item—fish, meat, poultry, vegetables fruits, et al—is listed at the bottom. The customer feels he is getting top quality since the supplier attaches his name to it; conversely, the supplier feels compelled to provide the best.

By its placement of items and graphic treatment, a menu can influence decision making and help order a meal. If each course, from aperitif through hors d'oeuvre, entree, vegetable, salad and dessert, is listed, the customer is more apt to select from each category instead of opting only for the entree. Or, if a restaurant wants to emphasize its full course dinners as opposed to *à la carte* ordering, it can do that too with the menu. Take Windows on the World. Here, the left side of the menu, devoted to the courses in the dinner offering is clearly designed to attract the reader's eye and hold it. The type face is larger than it is for the *à la carte* listing on the right page and easier to read; also, the interplay of typography and white space suggests that dinner items receive special attention in the kitchen. The *à la carte* listings, by contrast, seem less important and included only as an accommodation.

What else can a successful graphics program achieve? It can help establish a strong identity for a restaurant through repetition of the logo. Or, if a restaurant's marketing program calls for it to be trendy with a limited life span, a graphic treatment can help portray the idea. Says Glaser: "There are certain kinds of typography and design that last for three years; there are others that last for ten years. It all depends on the overall scheme."

There is no hard and fast checklist to follow as a guarantee to success. The only rule is that of clarity and readability, and here considerations such as the type of lighting and the average age of the prospective audience come into play as much as the type face, point size and leading. After clarity, Glaser alludes to only one other rule: that the graphics be appropriate to the situation. It's not a question of their being fancy or expensive." The worst way to use graphics? "As a substitute for poor food and service," is the reply.

MILTON GLASER is a designer, teacher and author of *Milton Glaser: Graphic Design.*

The menu, dessert menu and wine list for the Crystal Pavilion in Crown Center, Kansas City, help establish a color story for the restaurant. The logotype for Windows On The World, New York City, is repeated on all menus. The bold colors and logo design for Sneakers, a luncheon club in Florida, contribute to the desired theme of informality. The careful attention given to the menu for the Blue Ribbon Delicatessen at Crown Center implies that the same care is devoted to the deli fare.

Menu Designs

A menu is essentially a listing of dishes and drinks. But it is much more than that. It illustrates the personality of the restaurant, often being a major contributor to that personality. A menu is sometimes the work of the restaurant's interior designer, sometimes the work of a graphic designer chosen by the interior designer, but—at all times—it must be complementary to the restaurant's decor.

The following examples are from an exhibition held at the New York Art Directors Club. It was produced by Judi Radice, promotion manager at Rapp & Collins, the direct marketing agency of Doyle Dane Bernbach. Her idea for the show was inspired by Rizzoli's book *Menu Designs*.

Jamboree Restaurant, New York
*Designed by TVR Menus & More/
Tom Vlahakis*

Tucano Restaurant, New York
Courtesy of Michael Weeks

Maison Prunier Restaurant, Paris
Dated 1929
Courtesy Monica Geran

MS Europa, Hapag-Lloyd
Bremen, W. Germany
Designed by Barbara Geissler
Courtesy Rizzoli N.Y.

Book cover "Menu Designs"
Rizzoli International Publications
New York City

Gualtiero Marchesi Restaurant, Milan
Designed by Giorgio Lucini
Courtesy Rizzoli N.Y.

Café Tuileries, Hotel Continental, Paris
Designed by Akila/Pasquet/Pantin
Courtesy Rizzoli N.Y.

Trumpet's Restaurant, New York
Courtesy of Strathmore Paper Co.

Palace Hotel Grill, St. Moritz
Designed by Walter Gammeter
Courtesy Rizzoli N.Y.

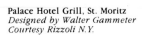

SETTIMANA GASTRONOMICA
VENEZIANA
presentata dal
GRITTI PALACE
Febbraio 1979

GRILL PALACE HOTEL ST. MORITZ

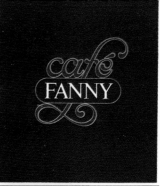

Café Fanny, The Biltmore Hotel, N.Y.
Designed by Milton Glaser

Fiorello's Restaurant, West Side, N.Y.
Designed by Milton Glaser

Port of Italy Restaurant,
Temple Hills, Maryland
Designed by Lola Lehrman
Design Unlimited/Culinary Concepts

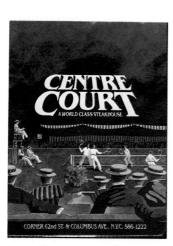

Café Olé Restaurant, Boise, Idaho
Designed by Dennis Chase

RJ's Restaurant, Beverly Hills, California
Courtesy Sal Casola

Yesterday's Restaurant,
Westwood, California
Designed by Design Dynamics

The Great House Towers of Quayside,
Miami
Designed by Milton Glaser

Centre Court Restaurant, New York
Designed by Lee Corey Studio/
Rhoda Harris

Saffron Restaurant, New York
Courtesy of Strathmore Paper Co.

205

David Winfield Willson on Lighting

Restaurant lighting should perform two major functions: (1) it must enhance the mood established by the design of the interior and the type of food service to be offered, and (2) diners must be able to comfortably read the menu and see their meal (and one another) in the most attractive way possible. Everyone has dined in restaurants where guests at one table might be seated under a harsh downlight, while those at another table can barely see. This usually results from using recessed downlight fixtures that have been placed too far apart and, in an effort to build up the *general* light level, using lamps of too high wattage in the fixtures. To make matters worse, the lens of the lamp is often right at the opening of each fixture, so that glare from the lamp hits the eye, creating visual contrast that is highly uncomfortable and that makes it more difficult to see well.

One doesn't need a great deal of light for the task of reading a menu and seeing food adequately, as long as there isn't the kind of visual contrast that distracts the eye. After all, one *can* read a newspaper under cloudless moonlight. The iris of the eye opens to full in such a case, and one can see surprisingly well in such a low light level. If the iris is caused to shrink (to become smaller) because of a bright light source in the near vicinity, however, then the eye can't take in enough light with which to read the newsprint. The same condition occurs in a restaurant setting when one sits in a dimly lighted area but encounters glare from light sources in the ceiling, such as exposed downlight lamps or bare-bulbed chandeliers. Those sources may not be near enough to light the menu well, but the glare can still cause shrinking of the iris. If one is sitting under a bright light source and tries to see into an adjacent dimly lighted area, the problem is the same.

The foundation of restaurant lighting should be a general quality of light that is relatively even over the entire space, with no pockets of excessive visual contrast. The level of the general lighting can be high or low, according to the atmosphere to be established in the space, and once that foundation is laid, accent or focal lighting can be added to heighten the mood. As long as it is all kept in balance, no one will have a problem reading a menu. Even if each table is lighted individually, there should still be an overall glow of general lighting, so that there is no uncomfortable visual contrast between the table and other areas of the space. There are many ways to produce general lighting. Probably the most common are indirect sources, such as uplight from soffits around the room, and/or direct downlight from recessed fixtures. Indirect soffit light is more difficult to use, for the walls of a space can't be too far apart nor the soffits too close to the ceiling, or else the light will not spread enough to sufficiently illuminate the middle of the space. Recessed downlights can produce an excellent quality of general lighting, as long as they are used properly. First of all, the fixtures should be deep enough to have at least a 45-degree visual cut-off of the lamp to the eye—more, if possible. Secondly, they should be spaced close enough together so that their beams will criss-cross each other, as in sketch on page 208.

With criss-crossing beams, harsh shadows, such as those caused on the face under bright downlight, are eliminated. In an average ceiling height of 9 feet, the fixtures should be on no more than 4-foot centers (i.e., not farther than 4 feet apart). While this generally entails the use of more fixtures than we've perhaps been accustomed to using, the wattage of each fixture can be consider-

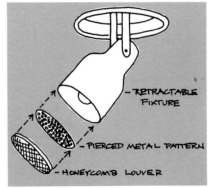 

CAPISTRANO'S, Burlingame, California
Interior designer: Nancy Constanino
Photographer: Steven Fridge

Retractable light fixtures, made by Halo Lighting, were converted to cast the shadow patterns on the wall. Nova louvers, combined with patterns cut from pierced aluminum grille, were placed at the open end of each fixture (the grille is available in 3' × 3' sheets from most builder supply and hardware stores). 200-watt clear lamps were used for the wall patterns, and the same fixtures and louver/grille combination were used, with 150-watt clear lamps, to provide dappled general downlight throughout the restaurant. Only clear lamps (not frosted) will produce pattern effects such as this.

ably reduced, because one has produced an even wash of light over everything, which is easy on the eye, thereby removing the uncomfortable visual contrasts that make it necessary to pump more wattage into the space to be able to see.

In my own work, I rarely use lamps of more than 30 watts for general lighting in restaurants and, at that, I know I'll be dimming them substantially to bring the light down to a comfortable level. In addition, the need for less wattage per lamp can allow one to use smaller size lamps and, therefore, fixtures with smaller visible apertures. For example, a fixture to house a 150 watt R40 lamp would have an aperture of around 6" The aperture of a typical fixture to house a 75 watt R30 lamp would generally run around 5" (though Lightolier makes one, their No. 7058, with an aperture of

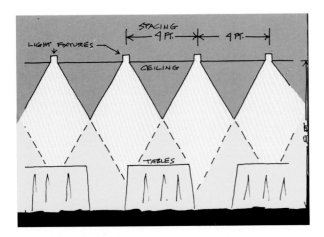

only 3¾"). When using standard voltage fixtures, a very interesting version for general lighting is the pinhole downlight, with a visible aperture of only 2". It should be used *only* if it has been designed to take an ER lamp, however. (An ER lamp has an elliptical reflector that focuses the light beam 2" ahead of the lamp, instead of spreading the light immediately; the use of *any* lamp but an ER in a pinhole fixture would be wasteful of energy, since much of the light output from a conventional reflector lamp would be trapped inside the fixture.) Pinhole fixtures for ER lamps can be difficult to find (Capri Lighting makes one, their No. R15X-R20P, which has an adjustable socket so that any size ER lamp, from a 50 watt ER30 to a 120 watt ER40, can be used).

Low voltage downlight fixtures are another choice for general lighting in restaurants. I prefer to use a fixture that takes a 13-volt No. 1383 R12 lamp, for I find its 20 watts and wide beamspread ample for the light level required in most restaurant interiors. The relatively new 12-volt MR16 lamps are the latest rage, but I don't favor them for general lighting. (Mind you, this is a personal

THE MIRABEAU RESTAURANT, Oakland, California
Interior designers: Baldwin/Clark Associates
Photographer: Stephen Fridge

Light images from Mini-ellipse projectors, by Berkey Colortran, are used as art in the cocktail lounge, shown here, as well as in the main dining room. Recessed low voltage fixtures, by Alesco, with 20 watt R12 lamps, provide the general downlighting. Since the restaurant is in the Kaiser Aluminum headquarters building, it seemed appropriate to the author to use Kaiser foil, with pin-prick holes and small razorblade cuts, to fabricate the delicate patterns used in the projectors.

opinion.) The widest beamspread available in MR16 lamps is only about 40 degrees wide, which means that at table height, from a ceiling of 9 feet, the beam would cover only about 5 feet in diameter, and the beam has a definite hard edge, instead of feathering out softly as the beams of the R and ER lamps do. MR16 fixtures would, then, have to be used closer together in order to create a soft overall light with no drop-off between fixtures. MR16 lamps also produce a tremendous amount of glare, if not used in a fixture that protects the eye from seeing it.

Where the MR16 lamp shines, as it were, is in its use for accent or focal lighting. The lamp is only 2" in diameter, so the fixture to house it can be quite compact. Once the foundation of good general lighting has been laid, especially if fixtures with small apertures have been used, it's marvelous to be able to light art and accessories with recessed focal-light fixtures that also have small apertures. The newest sensation in recessed MR16 fixtures is a trim from Capri, with a small mirror-scoop that lowers through a 1¼" square aperture, so that the lightbeam can be focused right up to the ceiling. A conventional recessed focal-light fixture would be limited to placement

HOLDIAY INN, Oklahoma City, Oklahoma
Interior designer: Larry Williams
Photographer: David Winfield Willson

Focusable recessed fixtures, by Capri Lighting, with low voltage MR16 lamps, are used to light table-tops and decorative objects in the cocktail lounge (shown here) and throughout the adjoining dining room and coffee shop. Other Capri fixtures, for 20 R12 low voltage lamps, cast a soft overall downlight in the three spaces. Strips of Plugmold, with plug-in nightlights, are used behind the three paintings to create a halo-effect. The 7' × 7' paintings, by the author, become backgrounds after dark for projection of abstract images from a pair of slide projectors opposite each painting. These, housed in the soffit of the skylight, together with a computer controller to synchronize all six projectors, slowly dissolve the projected images, one into another. A total of 486 slides are used and the program runs for 2 hrs., 40 min. before it repeats itself.

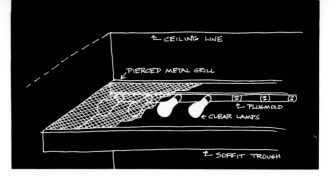

no more than 1½" to 2 feet from the wall on which an object is to be lit, in a 9-foot ceiling situation. Located any farther from the wall, the lightbeam wouldn't be able to reach art hung at normal height. The mirror fixture, however, with its wide focusing range, can be placed farther out from the wall, where the beamspread of any MR16 lamp will be more effective. There are a variety of MR16 lamps available, in wattages of 20 to 75, but they fall basically into only four general categories of beamspread sizes: floodlamps, with beamspreads of about 38 to 40 degrees; medium spotlamps, with beamspreads of about 24 degrees; narrow spotlamps, with beamspreads ranging between 12 and 17 degrees; and two new lamps from GE, one with an 8-degree beamspread and the other with a beamspread of 6 degrees. The slight difference of degrees of beamspread in each category is almost meaningless to the eye. The beamspreads of all MR16 lamps are round which can make it difficult to adequately light long shapes or objects at an extreme angle to the fixture. Capri, however, offers a round linear spread lens capable of elongating an MR16 beamspread at any angle and thus solving that problem. I caution again that MR16 lamps produce a tremendous amount of glare if not properly controlled; it's imperative that a louver be used in any MR16 focal-light fixture.

Dimming

Focal lighting makes it own contribution to the general light level in a space by sending back ambient light reflected from art and objects being lighted. The accumulative total of light produced by general and focal lighting will be greater than one might expect, even using low-wattage lamps. One must have the capacity to lower the total light to the proper level and, of more importance, to lower it selectively, so that all the lighting, general and focal, can be brought into balance. This means that it is mandatory that a dimming system be used, preferably with as many of the separate lighting circuits as possible controlled by individual dimmers, so that the lighting balance can be "fine tuned."

Even though a restaurant may receive natural light during the daytime, some areas in the space will still be dark enough to require artifical light, and that light will have to be at a higher level in the daytime—to hold its own against the very bright natural light—than it will in the late afternoon and after dark. This is particularly true if the space is relatively large and the natural light comes from only one side, for this situation, inevitably creates visually uncomfortable glare unless the lighting is balanced. If the restaurant is windowless, one must be careful not to make patrons walk from bright daylight into a "black hole" or, even worse, back out into a blast of light after dining. A lack of windows is no excuse for keeping a

Diagram shows Plugmold outlets on 6" centers installed in a light-trough. Used with clear lamps in socket adaptors and overlayed with pierced metal grille (see bottom illustration, page 206), they will produce the effect shown in photo 1. In photo 2, two colors of theatrical gel have been added. Photo 3 illustrates the reflection of a tight beam of light, such as a low voltage display spotlamp, which has been directed at crinkled metallized plastic from a hidden source.

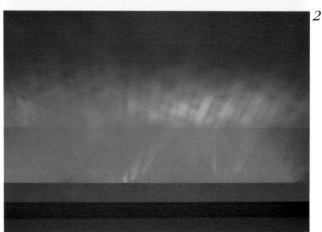

restaurant dark during the daytime. The interior lighting can be changed during the day so that diners have a sense of the time of day. Breakfast service should have the highest level of light, for single diners often read over their morning coffee. The light can be lowered somewhat for luncheon service, though it still shouldn't be a tremendous contrast psychologically to what one knows is happening out-of-doors. The cocktail hour can be lower still, and dinner time can finally settle down to a more intimate level of light. If the restaurant encourages bar business after the dinner hour, that's the time to take the lighting to its *most* intimate level.

With or without windows, a restaurant interior should have changes of balanced light level during day and evenings, and dimmers are needed to accomplish these changes. Next, of course, comes the question of who is to set the dimmers and control the daily changes. Every restaurant employee, from management on down, will have his own opinion of what the light level should be at any given time of day, and one can bet one's bottom dollar that, if left exposed, the dimmers will be changed several times a day more than planned. Over time the light levels will be considerably altered from the original concept. The *only* insurance against this is the use of a pre-set dimming system. There are many excellent systems now being made that allow the designer to adjust the dimmers to any given combination of brightness for a particular effect, or "scene," then assign that scene to a numbered control button. Let's assume that button No. 1 would be the scene set for the breakfast hours and through the morning, button No. 2 for lunch through the start of the cocktail hour, etc. The individual dimmers are kept locked behind a panel with only a button exposed for each scene to be used during the day. This means, however, that someone must be responsible for making each change at the proper time. Better yet, if budget allows, is a system in which the change of scenes is controlled by time clocks, preferably astrological time clocks, which automatically adjust for the seasonal change of daylight hours throughout the year. Most of these systems can be adjusted so that each scene change takes place over several minutes and is undisturbing.

Special Effects Lighting

Going beyond the basic needs that lighting should fulfill, there are some wonderfully simple means to enhance the mood of a restaurant interior with lighting effects. Some can be used simply to underscore the overall lighting; others can become focal points of the interior in themselves.

Aberrations from the light of clear bare lamps can be purposely used to achieve an effect; Hytron makes a PAR38 Krypton reflector lamp that throws a very subtle dappled quality of light, because of its irregularly shaped lens, and the old-fashioned candle-flame lamps also throw a subtle and unique light, when the clear version is used. Light reflected from the surface of water or crinkled metalized plastic can be marvelous. All of these effects should be directed from hidden sources, however, so that light from the lamp never sends glare directly to the eye of the viewer.

When the interior justifies it, I love to use patterns of light, sometimes softly dappled, sometimes quite definite. Uplight through the leaves of plants is the most obvious example of light-and-shadow pattern, but similar effects can be less accidentally achieved and used to great advantage. Several means are illustrated in the accompanying photographs.

The most exciting and practical way to project light patterns for normal architectural use is with the new recessed "framing projector" made by Capri Lighting. It uses a 75 watt MR16, 12-volt lamp, and Capri offers a selection of stock patterns which can be put into the fixture to be projected; patterns can be custom-made to a designer's specification, as well. I most often use patterns slightly out-of-focus, to evoke the dappled look of moonlight through greenery, but patterns can also be exciting when projected, in focus, over three-dimensional surfaces, such as a wall sculpture, particularly if it has been designed for that purpose. Patterns projected onto the same surface from several sources can be quite effective, especially when done in subtly different colors. Once one begins to experiment with effects like these, countless new inspirations will occur.

Successful restaurant lighting is not difficult to achieve. If one puts oneself in the place of a patron, it's easy to determine what pitfalls to avoid and what problems to solve in order to make dining in the establishment a visual pleasure. Experimentation with fixtures *before* specifying them is mandatory insurance against making irrevocable mistakes on the job and toward finding the right lighting tools to achieve the quality of light—as well as the visual "look"—one is after. Then, after one has designed a good foundation of lighting into the space, it's time to take at least a small step toward trying something new in an area of the installation that won't be disastrous if it doesn't quite work as planned. Again, experimentation beforehand will be insurance against a total flop. That first small step can be a learning experience that leads to larger steps, and the sense of achievement in successfully executing a new concept in restaurant lighting is one that can't be equaled.

DAVID WINFIELD WILLSON is a lighting designer whose headquarters are in San Francisco. His work includes hotels, restaurants, retail stores and, especially, residences across the country, and his primary interest is in breaking ground with his use of unorthodox lighting techniques.

Warren Platner on Lighting

As the designer of some of our most famous restaurants (The American Restaurant in Kansas City and Windows on the World), Warren Platner has very definite ideas on lighting in general and on restaurant lighting in particular.

His first edict: don't try to light spaces; you can only light surfaces which, in turn, will light a space. "Surfaces" are specific task areas or features within a space such as tapestries, art objects, even flowers. He points to the dramatic entrance corridor at Windows on the World (see pages 14 and 15) as an example. By lighting the walls and ceiling with their mirrored and glass-faceted surfaces, he has, from the reflected light, lit the space and the people walking through it.

Another suggestion is to create a sculptural object which becomes one of the major sources of light in a room as he did in the American Restaurant (see examples on the facing page). Here the ceiling is turned into a decorative form with a canopy-like chandelier which helps to balance the natural lighting by day and to supplement the individual lighting over tables at night.

On the other hand, he warns, hanging "pretty" chandeliers as many designers are wont to do is a mistake, for more often than not they cast light in the wrong places. The same is true with the use of a ceiling "system;" some areas will have too much light and others not enough. Small table lights simulating candlelight are also to be avoided.

Incandescent lighting is best for use in restaurants, for colors don't look good under fluorescents—particularly pink and flesh tones. Nor does food: a rare steak will look gray, for example.

Incandescent lighting, although it produces more heat than light, creates a warm effect, like sitting by a fire or by candlelight.

The level of lighting in restaurants is also important: it should be high enough for people to be able to read the menu and see their food, but low enough to create a feeling of intimacy. Lower lighting levels can be used over bars which should be glamorous and cozy in feeling.

When artificial lighting has to compete with daylight, extra illumination is needed to counteract the natural element. Since artificial lighting behaves differently when mixed, dimmers are particularly important during transitional late-afternoon periods.

Shadows are important in lighting effects, for without them we have no perception of light. Too many designers are more concerned with what the lighting fixture looks like than with the quality of light it produces. Again, he points to the use of crystal chandeliers hanging from a ceiling.

By manipulating light very carefully, he maintains, it is possible to double or triple the power of an object—to create a three-dimensional quality and to dramatize form, color and shape—something which has been done in the theater for many years but has only recently been discovered by designers.

WARREN PLATNER, FAIA, is an internationally known designer of buildings, interiors, exhibitions, lighting and furniture. His outstanding restaurant designs include Windows on the World and the American Restaurant in Kansas City. His architectural/design offices are located in New Haven, Conn.

Lighting in the American Restaurant at Crown Center, Kansas City, comes from three major sources: outdoors, a canopy-like chandelier and individual lighting over tables inside. The ceiling light helps to balance the natural lighting by day and supplement the table lighting at night.

213

Paul Marantz on Lighting

Paul Marantz finds it difficult to translate lighting design into words. Lighting, he says, is an experiential and dimensional task, and he approaches it not from a product specification stance, but with an eye toward the effects he wants light to achieve. Regardless, he launches enthusiastically into the subject of lighting in restaurants.

"It seems to me," he begins, "to be a question of two issues, each equally weighted." First there is the matter of a scheme which pursues an idea or the theme of the space. All of the contributing images, both in the interior and the lighting design, must work within that particular framework. "The lighting should be at one with the imagery of the space. It has to be part of the total picture. But," he adds, "there is no one right way to light any room."

The second issue focuses on the sympathetic lighting of people—actually the lighting of people's faces since most of their bodies are hidden when seated. "The lighting should make people look as healthy and well turned-out as they try to be." After all, he explains, restaurants are part of the celebratory aspects of life, and people want to look good during these events.

Theories are fine, but how does one go about implementing them? Are there any hard and fast rules to follow? And conversely, are there any definite pitfalls to be easily avoided? Short of hiring an expert, what should a restaurant designer do about lighting?

Starting with the lighting of faces, Marantz likens his approach to that of lighting sculpture. Generally, he eschews direct overhead illumination. His maxims: the light should come from a lateral direction; it should come from a relatively large light source; the source should be placed fairly low in the room in relation to the seated person. Lateral light, he explains, is infinitely more flattering. A quick demonstration shows overhead lighting to produce deep shadows on some facial areas while washing out other sections—particularly below the eyes—with glaring highlights. Thus, Marantz relies heavily on a room's walls. He recommends using wall fixtures and sconces, illuminating wall-affixed objects, or using the wall as a reflective surface beaming overhead light there instead of on the diners below. He acknowledges, however, that this theory makes lighting a large room particularly difficult. In that case, he says, "the friendliest thing to do is put a candle or small lamp on individual tables, but given the size of most tables, this frequently becomes a barrier."

Aside from size, another difficulty arises in rooms with dark decor schemes. "The darker the room," says Marantz, "the more need for a diversity of small sources rather than a scarce amount of large sources." The reasoning? A dark room can never be light through reflection. So, one has to diversify the sources to prevent any one from being overwhelming. "A lighting designer," he comments, "has to respond to the palette."

After discussing his elementary concepts, Marantz adds that there are three variables in lighting: direction, intensity and color. Since the first factor already has been discussed, we address the latter two. Intensity has to do with establishing the right kinds of contrast (from indirect lighting to shadows) in order to model facial features. Contrast is especially important in a low-light restaurant during luncheon hours. "The eye needs time to adapt to changes in light level," he explains. Therefore, one must "step down" the illumination gradually through intervening rooms or vestibules. Patrons should not have to proceed from a bright street entry directly into a darkened dining room. As for a minimum quantity of light, according to Marantz, there is none. "People can eat happily in candlelight. It's a question of balance and difference in light levels.

The best color rendition, says the designer, comes from incandescent sources since they are essentially warm. "People can appreciate low levels of warm light as opposed to a higher level from cool sources." What about the related question of colored gels, we ask. After all, it's commonly accepted that people look best bathed in pink or peach light. Marantz, though he gives credence to the hypothesis, does not favor gels. It poses, he says, "a truth in packaging question. I prefer to take colored walls and change [through reflection] the color of light that is true." The principal caveat

LE CYGNE, New York, New York
Interior Designers: Voorsanger & Mills

The second floor dining room of this newly renovated restaurant is reached via a dramatic open stairwell. Since it was not possible to add windows to the room, lighting is through artificial means. Here, the main source is the 13'8' ceiling vault filled with backlit panels of fine mesh screen. "We wanted to create a luminous vault," says Marantz. It was not to be a skylight, but it was, he says, to create "an abstraction of light."

in playing with colored light is that most of the commercial gel filters available are too crude—read too saturated. Color filters on glass are more expensive and harder to find, but provide a more discreet effect. "It's the only way," he says.

Marantz's favorite New York restaurant vis-à-vis lighting is the Four Seasons; Richard Kelly was the lighting designer. "It's absolutely splendid," he says. "It works well because the great preponderance of light is either filtered through the windows or reflected from the walls." Eighty per cent of the light, he says, is directed to the walls; the other lighting comes from focal points—light directed on the trees, fountain and pool. "There's a lot of light play—contrast and pools of light."

With no false modesty, he cites Le Cygne as another choice. Newly renovated, with lighting designed by his firm, the restaurant is lit entirely from concealed sources—cove lighting and a vaulted luminous ceiling on the second floor providing indirect illumination throughout. The interesting problem here, he says, was to make the experience of going upstairs so wonderful that people would not object to dining on the upper level. The solution, he says, may have been overly successful; management reports a surfeit of requests for the upstairs room.

Understandably, Marantz believes that in restaurant design, lighting is as important a component as the linen, the table setting, the china, the waiters' uniforms, et al. In places where lighting consideration has been given short shrift, he takes it as a sign of indifference on the part of the restaurateur and the designer. It's as if nobody cared, and it is this that most irks him about the subject. But, we counter, he is sensitive to the matter. Take the average person. Is he aware of good, bad or even indifferent lighting? Marantz thinks yes–not necessarily on a conscious level, due perhaps, to a lack of training, but, he says, "in the creation of an environment, it's the refinement of all those details that make it special." And people are aware of those details, lighting included.

"Just as lighting is used to reveal things," he says in conclusion, "it can also be used to conceal things. Lighting is about making choices, establishing a hierarchy. In determining which elements to light, in making these choices, we are structuring the way in which the environment is seen. In doing so, we control the eye of the viewer."

PAUL MARANTZ, with training in architecture, architectural history and industrial design as well as lighting, brings a multi-disciplinary background to his work. He received his B.A. degree from Oberlin College and did graduate work at Case/Western Reserve University. He is currently adjunct associate professor of architecture at Columbia University, and is a member of the Illuminating Engineering Society, the United States Institute for Theater Technology, and the International Association of Lighting Designers. He is the recipient of seven Illuminating Engineering Society Lumen citations.

Cyril M. Harris on Acoustics

Some time ago, a famous New York bistro, concerned about the high noise level in its convivial quarters, asked me what measures it might take to reduce this. I lunched there, enjoying the cheerful ambiance as always but this time casting a scrutinizing eye over the interior design to see whether it would adapt to acoustical noise reduction measures. Indeed it could—I could have made it as quiet as a funeral home—but I also recognized that a major factor in the bistro's popularity was the very hubbub that was worrying its owners. The habitués kept returning because they relished the sense it gave them of being in the center of where things were happening. Don't change a thing, I told the owners. They didn't—and it flourishes still as crowded and as noisy as ever.

So quiet, as this incident indicates, is not always a virtue. But it is true that more often than not, people do prefer a sense of tranquility when they dine out, and restaurants that keep background noise levels down, avoid the jarring clatter of dishes and silverware, and are designed so that customers can enjoy a reasonable sense of privacy as they converse with their dining companions, find that these qualities are valuable assets. In fact, the noted New York restaurant critic Mimi Sheraton, notes unduly high noise levels in her reviews; among the amenities customers of quality establishments are entitled to expect, Ms. Sheraton feels, is a reasonable degree of tranquility.

If the goals are this sense of tranquility without hush; a perception of activity and popularity without intrusiveness or overcrowding; sufficient background noise to ensure privacy of conversation at each table but not so much that diners must raise their voices to be heard—how are these to be achieved? One elementary way is to allow considerable space between tables, but this is a luxury in an era of staggering per-square-foot rents and few restaurants can afford it. Architects and designers need to rely on other ways to control noise.

There are two principal methods of control: (1) increasing the acoustical absorption in the interior space, for noise levels diminish as the amount of absorption in the space is increased; and (2) isolating exterior noise, thereby preventing or limiting its transmission into the room.

Increasing Absorption Through Furnishings

Properly selected furnishings in an interior space can contribute significantly to the overall sound absorption in a room, and thus reduce the general background noise within it. Carpeting is particularly helpful, where practical considerations permit its use, because it not only supplies such absorption, but also reduces footfalls.

There are several guidelines to follow in selecting carpeting to achieve maximum noise control. *The greater the face weight (i.e., the weight per unit area of the carpet pile), the greater the sound absorption.* This means that *absorption increases with pile height, assuming all other characteristics of the carpet are the same.* Or, if the pile height is constant, the sound absorption increases with the density of weave, since this also increases the face-weight. The weight of the backing material is not important in this respect; it is faceweight that counts. And though cost obviously goes up with an increase in faceweight, it is important to recognize that the wearing qualities of the carpet also increase. Wearability also is improved if underlayment is used. Since such padding increases the overall thickness, it increases the sound absorption significantly, as illustrated in *Figure 1*, but this increase applies only if the underlayment is porous. You must be able to blow through it; nonporous padding is acoustically ineffective.

Furniture's usefulness in reducing noise levels in an interior space depends on the materials used in its construction. To provide significant sound absorption, the fabric used to cover it must be porous so that sound waves can penetrate the surface Similarly the padding beneath the fabric must be porous. Therefore, if a sponge Neoprene is used, it must be of the "open cell" type.

Draperies made of porous fabrics can be effective noise reducers if specific guidelines are followed. (1) In general, the heavier the fabric, the greater the absorption; very sheer draperies provide little sound absorption; (2) The greater the "percent fullness," the greater the sound absorption. Percent fullness is the percentage by which the width of the fabric exceeds the width of the finished drapery, i.e., 100% fullness indicates that the width of the material used is twice the width of the finished drapery (see *Figure 2*). (3) The absorption provided by a drapery is greater if it is spaced several inches away from a wall than if it is hung flat against it.

Use of Acoustical Materials

Architects and designers should keep in mind certain basic facts about the application of acoustical materials in interior spaces. For example, an acoustical material which is suspended from a ceiling, or otherwise spaced away from it, provides somewhat greater sound absorption than the same material cemented directly to the ceiling slab. Therefore, there is an acoustical advantage in mounting the material on furring strips or in using a suspension system, rather than cementing it directly onto the ceiling, as shown in *Figure 3*.

Designers and architects often do not like the appearance of many commercially available acoustical materials. They should recognize that they can put together their own combinations of materials which will not only meet their aesthetic requirements but may also be even more effective in reducing noise than the standard acoustical tiles. In general, such constructions make use of a fiberglass board or "blanket" (these are really the same, but the term "blanket" is usually applied to lower-density materials having no rigidity, so they can be rolled). Owens-Corning Type 703 Insulation and Duct Liner Board are examples of materials suitable for this purpose. These, and any similar materials, should be specified with a Neoprene face coating which prevents the fibers from coming loose.

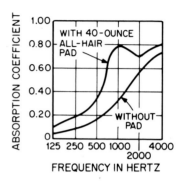

Figure 1. *The sound absorption of a loop pile, tufted carpet, with and without an underlayment. The padding increases the sound absorption significantly.*

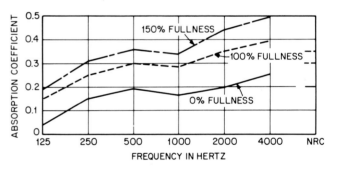

Figure 2. *The sound absorption provided by one type of draperies, hung with various percentages of fullness. Using increased fullness greatly increases the sound absorption provided.*

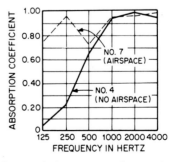

Figure 3. *The sound absorption coefficient of the same type of acoustical ceiling tile—with and without an airspace behind the tile. The airspace has the effect of increasing the sound absorption of the material, particularly for low pitched sounds.*

217

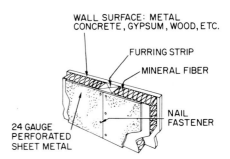

Figure 4. *A practical sound absorptive construction that can be cleaned repeatedly without loss of sound absorptive qualities.*

Since sound-absorptive materials such as fiber-glass have relatively little mechancial strength, if they are used as wall treatments, where they are vulnerable to physical abuse—whether the prodding of an inquisitive customer's fingers or the rough handling of cleaning staff—they must be protected by a covering such as perforated sheet-metal or metal mesh, perforated plywood, or perforated cement-asbestos board, as illustrated in *Figures 4, 5* and *6*. In general, the open area of such protective coverings should be at least 15 to 25% of its surface to maintain adequate sound absorption.

Neoprene face-coated fiberglass can be used on ceilings without a protective coating since its surface is safely distant from mechanical abuse, so there is considerably more freedom in design. An example of such design is to use wood strips across it, spaced ⅜ to ½ inch apart so as to expose a fraction of the fiberglass board to the room below. If the ceiling is very high, the designer may want to suspend some type of grid to provide the visual effect of a lower ceiling. In such cases, the fiberglass board may be attached directly to the ceiling with "stick clips" and the grid suspended below it.

When a ceiling is very high, acoustical materials affixed to it or attached with stick clips may still not reduce the noise level sufficiently; most of us have been in restaurants where we have been able to see this kind of treatment above, yet found the noise level obtrusive. The cause is the way in which sound waves behave when the ceiling is high and the side walls are hard; the sound bounces back and forth between the walls, with little of it absorbed by the ceiling treatment. In rooms with this kind of structure, it is advisable to mount acoustical treatment on the side walls as well. It can be of the protective-covered Neoprene fiberglass board described above, or of carpeting—although as indicated earlier, carpet does not provide very much sound absorption (except at high frequencies) unless it is backed with a porous, sound absorptive material. One type of mate-

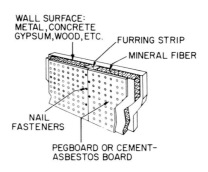

Figure 5. *This sound absorptive construction can take considerable abuse and can be repainted without loss of sound absorptivity if the holes of the perforated protective material are not covered with paint.*

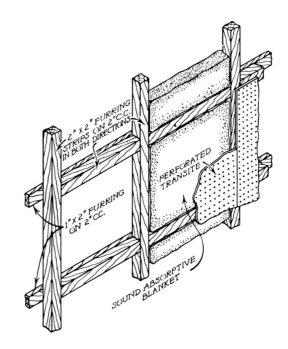

Figure 6. *An acoustical treatment consisting of a sound absorptive blanket covered by perforated cement-asbestos board.*

Figures 1, 2, 3, 4 and 5 reproduced from *Handbook of Noise Control*, Cyril M. Harris (Editor), McGraw-Hill, © 1979. Figure 6 reproduced from *Acoustical Designing in Architecture* by Vern O. Knudsen and Cyril M. Harris, Acoustical Society of America © 1978.

rial that is useful in combination with carpeting in wall treatments is fabricated of wood fibers and cement (e.g., Tectum), because it has considerable mechanical strength and will give the carpet support on the wall if it is subject to impact.

Isolating Exterior Noise

Kitchen noise. If a kitchen is sufficiently distant from the dining area, kitchen noise is not a problem, but this is not the case in many restaurants. The simplest way to deal with this is to *reduce the noise at its source,* by installing acoustical material in the kitchen itself. The material must be of a type that is not damaged by high humidity, and it must be capable of being cleaned and repainted, repeatedly without loss of acoustic quality; perforated metal pan tiles backed by sound absorptive material are an example. Treatment like this will reduce the clatter of pots and pans, but it will not eliminate it altogether.

It is often assumed that kitchen noise will be blocked by the doors that separate the kitchen from the dining room. This is not the case—particularly since the doors may be open a large fraction of the time. An effective means of dealing with this is to use a so-called "sound lock" between the kitchen doors and the dining area. A sound lock is a short corridor or vestibule (say 8 to 10 feet long) which is treated with highly efficient sound-absorptive material on its side walls and ceiling (such as a 2-inch blanket of fiberglass, covered with perforated plywood, as in *Figure 5*).

Air conditioning noise. When an architect designs a restaurant, the mechanical specifications should include a maximum permissible noise level in the unoccupied space with the air conditioning equipment in operation. This specification ensures that the noise from the mechanical system, and the noise generated from the grille, are both reduced to an acceptable level as they enter the dining room. But what can be done if the system is already installed and is too noisy? This can be a complex problem, not always soluble; but two

simple adjustments should be tried. The first is to adjust the angle of the louvers which control the angle at which air leaves the air outlet. The smaller the angle of deflection of the airflow, the less will be the noise which is produced. Another adjustment at, or near, the air outlet can affect the amount of air which flows through the outlet, by changing the position of the "damper" which controls this flow. Noise is produced as the air flows past the damper, and is least when the damper is in the *open* position—the position which permits the maximum amount of air to flow through the outlet grille. As the damper is positioned to decrease the airflow, the noise level increases; so the trick is to adjust the control so as to reduce noise to a minimum without producing objectionable drafts.

As can be seen, effective noise control measures in restaurants may be extensive and expensive; the scope of such treatments depends on the seriousness and the source of the problem. But lesser measures should not be overlooked in evaluating it either. Trays and serving tables can be made of materials that do not clatter; tablecloths—especially when used with underpads—help reduce impact noise; staff can be trained to handle plates and silverware deftly. Such practices improve the customers' perception of the courtesy and service that the restaurant is offering them. Leaving with a sense that dining there has been pleasurable, they are likelier to return in the future.

DR. CYRIL M. HARRIS, a physicist who specializes in acoustics, is Professor of Architecture and Electrical Engineering at Columbia University. He was the Acoustical Consultant for all the halls of the Kennedy Center in Washington, D.C., Orchestra Hall in Minneapolis, Powell Symphony Hall in St. Louis, Symphony Hall in Salt Lake City, the Metropolitan Opera House, the final reconstruction of Avery Fisher Hall, and the reconstruction of the New York State Theater at Lincoln Center in New York City. He is the recipient of many honors, including the American Institute of architects A.I.A. Medal; and he is a member of both the National Academy of Sciences and the National Academy of Engineering.

Directory of Interior Designers

ALLEMAND, DENIS
Denis Allemand Associates
8090 West Selma Ave.
Los Angeles, CA 90046
(213) 656-8944

ANDREWS, JOHN RICHARDS
Andrews, Chatelain/Architects
5200 Wisconsin Ave., NW
Washington, D.C. 20015
(202) 362-4500

BOXENBAUM, CHARLES
Boxenbaum, Architect
1860 Broadway
New York, NY 10023
(212) 586-5778

BRETOS, MARCEL
Marcel G. Bretos, Inc.
300 E. 33rd St.
New York, NY 10016
(212) 532-8329
and
787 N.E. 71st St.
Miami, FL 33138
(305) 758-6582

BROMLEY/JACOBSEN
242 West 27th St.
New York, NY 10001
(212) 620-4250

BRONSTEIN, EDWIN
Edwin Bronstein Associates
323 South Juniper St.
Philadelphia, PA 19107
(215) 732-7818

BUMGARDNER ARCHITECTS
51 University St., Suite 300
Seattle, WA 98101
(206) 223-1361

CALDER, NICHOLAS
348 E. 58th St., Suite 2B
New York, NY 10022
(212) 308-6670

CATAFFO, LOUIS
Intradesign
717 N. La Cienega Blvd.
Los Angeles, CA 90069
(213) 652-6114

CHICAGO ART & ARCHITECTURE
410 South Michigan Ave.
Chicago, IL 60605
(312) 922-2410

COSNER, JACK
1029 Orleans Ave.
New Orleans, LA 70116
(504) 522-6091

CREATIVE ENVIRONS
    of Lynn Wilson Associates, Inc.
4041 Laguna Ave.
Coral Gables, FL 33146
(305) 442-4041

D'AURIA, JAMES
12 West 27th St.
New York, NY 10001
(212) 725-5660

DONGHIA ASSOCIATES
315 East 62nd St.
New York, NY 10021
(212) 838-9100

ELIAS, BRAD
Hochheiser-Elias Design Group Inc.
322 East 86th St.
New York, NY 10028
(212) 535-7437

END, HENRY/ARAK, MICHAEL
Henry End/Michael Arak Associates
2600 Douglass Rd.
Suite 601
Coral Gables, FL 33134
(305) 445-2122

FELDERMAN, STANLEY
Stanley Felderman Ltd.
8584 Melrose Ave.
Los Angeles, CA 90069
(213) 855-0300

FERNANDEZ, WALDO
1754 Sunset Plaza Drive
Los Angeles, CA 90069
(213) 652-7303

FRANZEN, ULRICH
Ulrich Franzen Associates
228 East 45th St.
New York, NY 10017
(212) 557-6700

HAIL, ANTHONY
1055 Green St.
San Francisco, CA 94133
(415) 928-3500

HASSMAN, GEOFFREY
231 East 51st St.
New York, NY 10022
(212) 593-1455

HIRSCH/BEDNER
3216 Nebraska Ave.
Santa Monica, CA 90404
(213) 829-9087

HURD, KENNETH E.
Kenneth E. Hurd and Associates
Box 287
Lincoln Center, MA 01773
(617) 526-3434

INTERIOR CONCEPTS
468 Park Ave. South
New York, NY 10016
(212) 532-6767

I.S.D., INC.
305 East 46th St.
New York, NY 10017
(212) 751-0800

JENKINS, DENNIS
Dennis Jenkins Associates
5815 South West 68th St.
South Miami, FL 33143
(305) 662-2166

LEE, SARAH TOMERLIN
Tom Lee Ltd.
136 East 57th St.
New York, NY 10022
(212) 421-4433

LUGRIN/DUNDES DESIGN
80 Varick St.
New York, NY 10014
(212) 925-1070

MIRICH, SHELLY
Mirich Developments
1290 Homer St.
Vancouver, B.C. Canada V6B 2Y5
(604) 669-6939

PALATINUS, FRED
Palatinus Interior Design Inc.
239 East 18th St.
New York, NY 10003
(212) 473-7369

PARKER, KENNETH
Kenneth Parker Associates
The Granary
411 North 20th St.
Philadelphia, PA 19130
(215) 561-7700

PLATNER, WARREN
Warren Platner & Associates, Architects
18 Mitchell Drive
New Haven, CT 06511
(203) 777-6471

PLYLER, EDWARD C., ASID
428 North Washington St.
Alexandria, VA 22314
(703) 548-3600

RYBAR, VALERIAN
Valerian Rybar & Daigre Design Corp.
601 Madison Ave.
New York, NY 10022

THE SPACE DESIGN GROUP
8 West 40th St.
New York, NY 10018
(212) 221-7440

STOCKMAN, JUDITH
Judith Stockman Associates
111 Wooster St.
New York, NY 10012
(212) 925-1130

SYROP, ARNOLD
Arnold Syrop Associates, Architects
290 Fifth Ave.
New York, NY 10001
(212) 947-8530

TIHANY, ADAM
Adam Tihany International
57 East 11th St.
New York, NY 10003
(212) 505-2360

VILLANO, JOSEPH
Aquarius Design Ltd., Inc.
630 Wyckoff Ave.
Wyckoff, NJ 07481
(201) 891-3622

WALKER, KENNETH
The Walker Group
304 East 45th St.
New York, NY 10017
(212) 689-3013

WALZ, KEVIN
Walz Design Inc.
141 Fifth Ave.
New York, NY 10010
(212) 477-2211

ZAKAS, SPIROS
Zakaspace
252 Front St.
New York, NY 10038
(212) 732-0424

Directory of Photographers

ABRAHAM, RUSSELL
17 Brosnan Street
San Francisco, CA 94103
(415) 558-9100

ARDILES-ARCE, JAIME
633 Fifth Avenue
New York, N.Y. 10022
(212) 688-9191

BUSHER, DICK
7042 20th Place NE
Seattle, WA 98115
(206) 523-1426

CRANE, TOM
Darby and Marple Rds.
Haverford, PA 19041
(215) 525-2444

CSERNA, GEORGE
80 Second Avenue
New York, NY 10003
(212) 477-3472

FINE, ELLIOT
800 Carroll Street
Brooklyn, NY 11215
(212) 622-6613

FORER, DAN
1970 NE 149th Street
North Miami, FL 33181
(305) 949-3131

GEORGES, ALEXANDRE
66 Hilltop Circle
Palos Verdes, CA 90724
(213) 541-0033

HICKEY, L. BLAINE
Hickey-Robertson
1318 Sul Ross
Houston, TX 77066
(713) 522-7258

HILAIRE, MAX
560 Riverside Drive
New York, NY 10040
(212) 866-0533

HILL, JOHN
388 Amity Road
Bethany, CT 06525
(203) 393-0035

IDAKA, YUICHI
4100 West Irving Park Rd.
Chicago, IL 60641
(312) 282-7155

LEFCOURT, VICTORIA
1734 Linden Avenue
Baltimore, MD 21217
(301) 225-0405

LIEBERMAN, NATHANIEL (Studio, Ltd)
235 Warren St.
Brooklyn, NY 11201
(212) 855-9403

MCGRATH, NORMAN
164 West 79th Street
New York, NY 10024
(212) 799-6422

OTTE, GARY (Photographer Ltd.)
21-1551 Johnston St.
Vancouver, BC V6H 3R9
(604) 681-8421

PAIGE, PETER
Peter Paige Assoc., Inc.
37 West Homestead Avenue
Palisades Park, NJ 07650
(201) 592-7889

PORTER, WILLIAM A.
P.O. Box 6399
San Francisco, CA 94107
(415) 885-4840

REENS, LOUIS
4733 Crawford Drive
Box 88109
Lewisville, TX 75056
(214) 370-0119

ROBERTSON, OGDEN
Hickey-Robertson
1318 Sul Ross
Houston, TX 77066
(713) 522-7258

ROSS, MARK
345 East 80th Street
New York, N.Y. 10021
(212) 744-7258

STOLLER, EZRA
Esto Photographics
222 Valley Place
Mamaroneck, NY 10543
(914) 698-4060

TAYLOR, LARRY F.
Format Photography
P.O. Box 2641
Knoxville, TN 37901
(615) 522-7731

VITALE, PETER
157 East 71st Street
New York, NY 10021
(212) 249-8412

WHITE, CHARLES
115 South Mansfield Avenue
Los Angeles, CA 90036
(213) 937-3117

WINSTON, COURTNEY
70 West 83rd St., Duplex B
New York, NY 10024
(212) 496-6999

YOSHIMI, TOSHI
4030 Camero Avenue
Los Angeles, CA 90027
(213) 660-9403

Index

Restaurants and other Dining Facilities

Interviews and Special Features